How to Consciously Design Your Ideal Future

How to Consciously Design Your Ideal Future

BENJAMIN P. HARDY

Thought Catalog Books

Brooklyn, NY

THOUGHT CATALOG BOOKS

Copyright © 2016 by Benjamin P. Hardy

All rights reserved. Published by Thought Catalog Books, a division of The Thought & Expression Co., Williamsburg, Brooklyn. Founded in 2010, Thought Catalog is a website and imprint dedicated to your ideas and stories. We publish fiction and non-fiction from emerging and established writers across all genres. For general information and submissions: manuscripts@thoughtcatalog.com.

First edition, 2016

ISBN 978-1530227419

10 9 8 7 6 5 4 3 2 1

Cover design © KJ Parish

Dedicated to Mink Choi. Without her, this book wouldn't exist. Thank you for discovering my work, for valuing it, and for putting lots of work into editing and creating this book. I'm humbled by your generosity.

Contents

Praise for How to Consciously Design Your Ideal Future   ix
Introduction   xv

Part I. Organizing Your Life to Make Happiness, Health, and Success Automatic

1. Your Life May Be More Off-Course Than You Think   3
2. 8 Things Every Person Should Do Before 8 A.M.   17
3. Humans Are Holistic Systems: Your Physical Health Affects Everything   27
4. Ordinary People Seek Entertainment, Extraordinary People Seek Education   33
5. Expanding Your Time   37
6. No Other Success Can Compensate for Failed Relationships   49
7. Think and Grow Rich   57

Part II. Developing the Ability to Consciously Design Your Ideal Future

8. This Is How You Train Your Brain To Get What You Really Want   71
9. Mental Creation Always Precedes Physical Creation   77
10. Prayer, Meditation, and Visualization   83
11. Your Daily Journal—the Gateway to Your Future   87

Part III. Reframing Your Perceptual Reality

12. Gratitude—The Mother of All Virtues   103
13. There is No Way to Happiness   107

14.	Rapid Goal Achievement	113
15.	How to Create Enormous Value in the Work You Do	123
16.	Self-Acceptance Is The Counterintuitive Way To Become The Best Version Of Your Self	137

About the Author — 143

Praise for How to Consciously Design Your Ideal Future

"As Seneca once said, 'Life without a design is erratic.' Benjamin Hardy is one of my favorite young writers because he shows interesting and effective ways to organize and design our lives so that we can live and be how we wish."
—*Ryan Holiday, best-selling author of The Obstacle is the Way*

"In an age when few people think deeply about life, Benjamin Hardy is the exception. This collection of essays will challenge everything you think you know about yourself and the world around you and give you a practical plan for how to live the life you wish you had. Read it if you want to be better."
—*Jeff Goins, best-selling author of The Art of Work*

"Uncommonly thoughtful: that's what I think of when I read Benjamin Hardy's work. His is a roving curiosity, and it's a privilege for those of us who read him to see who he has read and thought about and engaged with. The result is the best kind of intellectual buffet: Benjamin draws on ancient thinkers, the latest research, poetry, and stories of all types to help us understand how we can be and do better. Get this book, and you'll be left, like I often am, grateful for having Benjamin Hardy in your life."

—*Jimmy Soni, editor at the Observer and author of Rome's Last Citizen: The Life and Legacy of*
Cato, Mortal Enemy of Caesar

"This book will not only provide you with practical advice on how to live your ideal life, but will help you reframe your psychology so that it's possible."
—*Emerson Spartz, one of the world's leading experts on internet virality, CEO of Dose, and the*
founder of MuggleNet, the #1 Harry Potter website

"Benjamin Hardy curates his most viral and influential pieces into one powerful 'little red book' that's destined to change lives and motivate readers to evolve by choice. Powerful, life-changing, and inspiring. 'Life is busy.' This is all too true. Making time to reader this book will change your life."
— *Lizzie Harwood, author of Xamnesia: Everything I Forgot in my Search for an Unreal Life*

"Your Ideal Future leaves you feeling inspired–like you have no choice but to commit to what you believe you should do. Read Hardy's book and discover a holistic approach to happiness, success and your ideal lifestyle."
—*Richie Norton, bestselling author of The Power of Starting Something Stupid*

"I am fascinated by all things performance. Every article

Benjamin writes challenges me stretch a little further and dig a little deeper. Now, imagine Benjamin's best work perfectly curated for you with incremental purpose. The result is Your Ideal Future."
—*Joe Jacobi, Olympic Gold Medalist and Performance Consultant*

"Whenever I read Benjamin's work I feel motivated, energized and hopeful about the future. The way he writes and encourages his readers lets us know that we have almost complete and utter control of our lives, the way we live and what we can expect. Always brilliant and very well researched."
—*Jane Barlow Christensen, CEO Barlow Herbal Specialties*

"Benjamin Hardy is the "Aristotle" of the millennial generation. Period."
—*Steve Down, President & Founder of Financially Fit, Even Stevens, The Falls Event Center,*
Blue Fish CE, and Storm Maker Media

"This book will literally change how you live and work. Benjamin is an amazing and passionate writer. The ideas in this book will help you reinvent yourself and design the future you want. It's never too late to start over. Everything you need to plan an amazing life has been covered by Benjamin. Your Ideal Future will guide you to find your true north."
—*Thomas Oppong, founder at All Top Startups, Curator at*

Postanly and Contributor at
Entrepreneur Magazine

"Insightful, motivational and necessary: Benjamin's understanding of the human passions will encourage you to design your future and teach you how to be intentional about your next steps."
—*Alba Lanuza, copywriter and blogger*

"One of the marks of a great writer is being able to make you think without making you think about the writing. Ben Hardy pulls this off terrifically in his new book. How to Consciously Design Your Ideal Future fulfills the promise of its title and will make you think differently about your work and life—in a beautiful way."
—*Shane Snow, CCO of Contently and best-selling author of Smartcuts: How Hackers, Innovators, and Icons Accelerate Success*

"Designing your life with intent is the best way to ensure you won't look back upon it with regret. This requires taking stock of who you are and what you do and making the changes to match who you want to be and what you want to do. "Just be yourself" is a terrible platitude for accepting the random attributes of character you've acquired thus far. Benjamin sets out to provoke thoughts that'll help you in this process. You don't need to agree with all the prescriptions to realize the value of considering them and picking what's right for you.

But giving them thought and consideration will be worth your time."

— *David Heinemeier Hansson, creator of Ruby on Rails, founder & CTO at Basecamp (formerly 37signals), NYT bestselling author of Rework*

Introduction

This book is a compilation of several articles I've written and published at Thought Catalog. The order of the content has been re-arranged, making the message cohesive and comprehensive. The purpose of this book is to radically adjust your perspective of yourself and life. Not only will your worldview be challenged in these pages, but also your daily behaviors and the way you approach your goals.

I wrote these articles between June and December of 2015. This was not an easy time of my life. Despite my wife and I both being graduate students, we had taken into our home three foster children (ages 4, 6, and 8). We love these kids as our own; but the sheer challenge has been humbling and crushing—often bringing us to our knees in search of answers.

I wondered if taking on such a responsibility would get in the way of my dreams to become a professional writer. To my surprise, the responsibility of caring for four people was a wake-up call. I could no longer wait for tomorrow to pursue my dreams. I had to take advantage of the little time I had while the kids were in school, *today*.

It may seem counterintuitive, but consciously engineering difficulty into your life may be exactly what you need. If you're not being challenged and growing, chances are you're stagnating and declining. As momentum-based beings, if we are in a state of decline, all areas of our lives suffer.

To increase my own personal commitment to my dreams,

in the Fall of 2015, I quit my university job and made writing my full-time work. This was my personal point of no return. No longer would I spend my waking hours completing other people's agendas. When you make a decision, the universe conspires to make it happen. The act of jumping-in with both feet utterly exposed my nakedness. I was forced to quickly improve, to take risks, and to become more than I currently was.

You are never pre-qualified to live your dreams. You qualify yourself by doing the work. By committing—even *over*committing—to what you believe you should do.

I wrote this book for myself. In these pages are things I'm trying to learn so I can personally improve my own life. If what I've written also helps and inspires you, all the better!

I challenge you to look beneath the words to the underlying principles and truths. Behind every principle is a promise.

Part 1

Organizing Your Life to Make Happiness, Health, and Success Automatic

1

Your Life May Be More Off-Course Than You Think

Despite turbulence and other conditions keeping airplanes off-course 90 percent of flight time, most flights arrive in the correct destination at the intended time.

The reason for this phenomenon is quite simple — through air traffic control and the inertial guidance system, pilots are constantly course-correcting. When immediately addressed, these course corrections are not hard to manage. When these course corrections don't regularly happen, catastrophe can result.

For example, in 1979, a passenger jet with 257 people onboard left New Zealand for a sightseeing flight to Antarctica and back. However, the pilots were unaware that someone had altered the flight coordinates by a measly two degrees, putting them 28 miles east of where they assumed to be. Approaching Antarctica, the pilots descended to give the passengers a view of the brilliant landscapes. Sadly, the incorrect coordinates had placed them directly in the path of the active volcano, Mount Erebus. The snow on the volcano blended with the clouds above, deceiving the pilots into thinking they were flying above flat ground. When the instruments sounded a warning of the quickly rising ground, it was too late. The plane crashed into the volcano and everyone onboard died.

An error of only a few degrees brought about an enormous tragedy.

Small things—if not corrected—become big things, always.

This flight is an analogy of our lives. Even seemingly inconsequential aspects of our lives can create ripples and waves of consequence—for better or worse.

- How are you piloting your life?
- What feedback are you receiving to correct your course?
- How often do you check your guidance system? Do you even have a guidance system?
- Where is your destination?
- When are you going to get there?
- Are you currently off-course? How long have you been off-course?
- How would you know if you are on the right course?
- How can you minimize the turbulence and other conditions distracting your path?

Organizing Your Life

I don't think I'm alone in being slightly scattered and sloppy about certain areas of my life.

Life is busy.

It's hard to keep everything organized and tidy. And maybe you don't want to have an organized life. But moving forward will require far less energy if you remove the excessive baggage and tension. Everything in your life is energy. If you're carrying too much—whether that's physical or emotional—your progress will be hampered.

In his book, *The 7 Habits of Highly Effective People*, Stephen Covey explains that some things are important, and some things are urgent. Most people spend their life prioritizing urgent and "shallow" activity (e.g., answering emails, putting out proverbial fires, and just day-to-day stuff). Very few people have organized their lives to prioritize almost exclusively important and "deep" activity (e.g., learning, health, relationships, travel, and goals).

No one cares about your success more than you do. If you're not a meticulous accountant about the important details of your life, then you aren't responsible enough to have what you say you want.

So how do you organize your life?

Environmental Energy

- Is your living space cluttered and messy or simple and neat?
- Do you keep stuff (like clothes) you no longer use?
- If you have a car, is it clean or just another place to keep your clutter and garbage?
- Does your environment facilitate the emotions you consistently want to experience?

- Does your environment drain or improve your energy?

Financial Energy

- Do you have unnecessary debt?
- Do you know how many dollars you spend each month?
- Do you know how many dollars you make each month?
- Are you making as much money as you'd like to be?
- What's holding you back from creating more value in other people's lives?

Most people don't track their expenses. But if they did, they'd be shocked how much money they waste on stuff like eating out. I'll be honest, as a creative and right-brained person, administrative and logistical details bog me down. I procrastinate and avoid them. But this lackluster behavior is holding me back from the very goals I'm trying to accomplish. Until I can hone in on my finances, I won't have a healthier financial life, regardless of my income. Until I take complete responsibility of my finances, I'll always be a slave to money.
    And so will you.

Relational Energy

- Are your relationships the most meaningful and enjoyable part of your life?

- Do you spend enough time nurturing the relationships that really matter?
- Do you maintain toxic relationships that no longer serve you?
- Are you authentic and honest in your relationships?

Like money, most people's relationships are not organized in a conscious manner. But with something so critical, we should take better stock of our relationships.

Health Energy

- Do you eat with the end in mind?
- Are you conscious of and in-control of the foods you put in your body?
- Does the food you eat improve or worsen the other areas of your life?
- Does your body reflect your highest ideals?
- Is your body as strong and fit as you want it to be?
- Are you healthier now than you were three months ago?

Health is wealth. If you're bed-ridden, who cares how organized the other areas of your life are? It's so easy to put our health on the side—like foregoing sleep, over-consuming stimulants, and making poor eating habits.

But little things become big things. And eventually everything catches up.

Spiritual Energy

- Do you have a sense of purpose in life?
- Have you come to terms with life and death in a way you resonate with?
- How much power do you have in designing your future?

When you organize your spiritual life, you become clear on what your life is about. You become clear on what you stand for, and how you want to spend each day. You develop conviction for what really matters to you, and what is a "distraction." No matter how well-defined, everyone has a moral system governing their behavior. Most people believe in being honest and good people. But until you organize your spiritual life, you'll experience internal conflict when acting contradictory to your values and vision.

Time

- How much of your time do you feel in complete control of?
- Is your time being wasted on things you don't intrinsically enjoy?
- Are the activities you spend your time doing moving you toward your ideal future?
- Are you spending most of your time furthering your own agenda or someone else's?
- What activities should you remove from your life?
- How much time do you waste each day?

- What would your ideal day look like?
- What activities could you outsource or automate that take up your time?

Until you organize your time, it will disappear and move quickly. Before you know it, you'll wonder where all the time went. Once you organize your time, it will slow down. You'll be able to live more presently. You'll be able to experience time as you want to. You'll control you're time rather than the other way around.

Stop What You're Doing and Get Organized

Getting organized and conscious of your present circumstances (e.g., your environment, finances, relationships, purpose, and time) puts you in a position to build toward the future you want. The fastest way to move forward in life is not doing more. It starts with stopping the behaviors holding you back. If you want to get in shape, you'll make more progress by stopping your negative behaviors than starting good ones. So, before you start exercising, purge the junk food from your diet. Until you stop the damage, you'll always be taking one step forward and one step backward.

Before you focus on making more money, reduce your spending. Detach yourself from needing more and become content with what you have. Until you do this, it doesn't matter how much money you make. You'll always spend what you have (or more). This is a matter of stewardship. Rather than wanting more, more, more — take proper care of what you currently have. Organize yourself. Dial it in. Your life is a garden. What good is planting if you don't prepare the soil and remove the weeds?

Why do most people stay stuck? They never organize. They try adding more, or being more productive, or taking a different approach. So before you "hustle," get organized.

Plan And Invest In Your Future

> "The best time to plant a tree was 20 years ago. The second best time is now." — Chinese Proverb

Taking these foundational areas of life and organizing them is essential to creating your ideal future.

Very few people consciously plan and design their life. It's actually startling how few Americans are investing in their future.

But you have complete power over the details of your life the moment you decide you're worthy of that power. That decision is manifest in tangible behaviors, like fixing or removing troubled relationships and saying "no" to activities that are nothing more than a waste of your time.

You get to decide right now.

> "If you fail to plan, you are planning to fail!" — Benjamin Franklin

Your vision should be based on your why, not so much your what. Your why is your reason, your what is how that is manifest. And your "what" can happen in a ton of different ways. For example, my why is to help people get clarity on the life they want to live, and to help them achieve their goals as quickly as possible. My what could be blogging, parenting, being a student, going out to dinner, and several other things.

Too many people think creating a vision is about nailing down exactly what they want in the next 20 years. The problem with this mega long-term approach to goal setting is that it actually slows your potential.

Instead of having a pre-set plan of what he wants to do, Tim Ferriss executes on 3–6 month experiments that he's currently excited about. He told Darren Hardy in an interview that he has no clue what the outcome of his experiments might be. So there's no point in making long-term plans. He has no clue what doors will open up, and he wants to be open to the best possibilities.

But his *why* never changes.

Invest in Your Future

When you choose to forego momentary gratification in order to have an enhanced future, you are investing in your future. Most people fail to do this successfully. Most people don't purposefully invest in their finances, relationships, health, and time. But when you invest in yourself—and in your future—you ensure your future present moments will continue to get richer and more enjoyable. Thus, your life will continue getting better and more in-line with your ideal vision.

Track Important Metrics

"When performance is measured, performance improves. When performance is measured and reported, the rate of improvement accelerates." — Thomas Monson

Getting organized and investing in your future are futile if you're not tracking. In regards to the most important areas of your life, you need to be on top of what's going on. Tracking is difficult. If you've tried it before, chances are, you quit within a few days. Research has repeatedly found that when behavior is tracked and evaluated, it improves drastically.

If you're not tracking the key areas of your life, than you're probably more off-course than you think. If you were to be honest with yourself, you'd be stunned how out-of-control things have become. As J.M. Barrie, author of *Peter Pan*, has said, "The life of every man is a diary in which he means to write one story, and writes another; and his humblest hour is when he compares the volume as it is with what he vowed to make it."

The cool part is, once you get organized, make a plan, and start tracking, desired change happens quickly.

The areas I'm personally tracking are:

- My income/expenses
- The amount of new email subscribers I get each month
- Every minute of my life (through a simple planner)
- My key relationships
- Daily progress toward my few goals

- My weight, muscle-mass, and body fat percentage each month
- You can track whatever priorities you have. But I can absolutely promise you that once you do, your conscious awareness of these things will increase. You're ability to control these things will enhance. Your confidence will wax strong. And your life will become simpler.

You'll be living a simple, yet organized and refined life. You'll be responsible, which put another way is freedom.

Prayer and Meditation To Reduce Noise

"I have so much to do today that I'm going to need to spend three hours in prayer in order to be able to get it all done." — Martin Luther

There's a lot of emphasis on hustle these days.

Hustle, hustle, hustle.

But all the hustle in the wrong direction isn't going to help you. Yes, by hustling you can fail often, fail fast, and fail forward. However, as Thomas Merton has said, "People may spend their whole lives climbing the ladder of success only to find, once they reach the top, that the ladder is leaning against the wrong wall."

This happens way too often. We get caught in the thick of thin things. Far too late do we realize that in our mad rush, we were pursuing someone else's goals instead of our own. But spending a large chuck of time in prayer and/or meditation does more than provide clarity to what you're doing. These things open your mind up to possibilities you can't get while busy. For example, a few days ago I spent the entire morning praying, thinking deeply, listening to inspirational music, and writing in my journal. A few hours into this process, an idea came to me that is absolute gold. I also got insights regarding important relationships during that time, which when those insights came in, I immediately sent out emails or texts to those people. Amazing collaborations and mentorships were the resultant outcome.

But there's more.

Your thoughts are incredibly powerful. They actually govern not only you but those around you. Think about it, if you think positively about the people you're around, their lives are better. This is why people "send positive energy" or pray for other people. It actually makes a difference.

Your thoughts create endless ripples—even waves—of consequence all around you.

While praying and/or meditating for a large portion of time, the level of your thoughts will elevate. And interesting things will begin happening. If you're uncomfortable with the idea of miracles, you can think of it as luck. Whatever you call it, when you spend large portions of time every day in deep reflection mode, luck strikes. Stuff happens that is completely outside of your control for your benefit.

For instance, during my deep dive into my mind and soul, one of my favorite authors came across my blog. He retweeted one of my articles and reached out to me. If you're skeptical of these ideas. Give it a try. Why do you think the majority of the world's most successful have rituals such as these? There is a higher realm you can tap into that unlocks limitless possibilities.

The only thing holding you back from those things is your mind.

Move Toward Your Goals Every Single Day

How many days go by where you did nothing to move toward your big goals?

Probably too many.

Life is busy.

If you don't purposefully carve time out every day to progress and improve—without question, your time will get lost in the vacuum of our increasingly crowded lives. Before you know it, you'll be old and withered, wondering where all that time went.

> *"You pile up enough tomorrows, and you'll find you are left with nothing but a lot of empty yesterdays."*–Harold Hill

After you've gotten yourself organized, made plans, started tracking, and gotten into the habit of prayer/meditation, taking action and hustling will be automatic. It's good practice to do these kind of things at the beginning of your day before your will power depletes.

If you don't, it simply will not get done. By the end of your day, you'll be exhausted. You'll be fried. There will be a million reasons to just start tomorrow. And you will start tomorrow — which is never.

So your mantra becomes: *The worst comes first. Do that thing you've been needing to do. Then do it again tomorrow.*

If you take just one step toward your big goals every day, you'll realize those goals weren't really far away.

It's really easy to get off-course in life. Like airplanes, we constantly need to make course-corrections. But we can ensure we get where we want in life by organizing ourselves, planning for our future, tracking our progress, heightening our mindset, and hustling. Do this long enough and you'll be shocked.

Go!

2

8 Things Every Person Should Do Before 8 A.M.

Life is busy. It can feel impossible to move toward your dreams. If you have a full-time job and kids, it's even harder.

How do you move forward?

If you don't purposefully carve time out every day to progress and improve—without question, your time will get lost in the vacuum of our increasingly crowded lives. Before you know it, you'll be old and withered, wondering where all that time went.

As Harold Hill has said: "You pile up enough tomorrows, and you'll find you are left with nothing but a lot of empty yesterdays."

Rethinking Your Life and Getting Out of Survival Mode

This article is intended to challenge you to rethink your entire approach to life. The purpose is to help you simplify and get back to the fundamentals.

Sadly, most people's lives are filled to the brim with the

nonessential and trivial. They don't have time to build toward anything meaningful.

They are in survival mode. Are you in survival mode?

Like Bilbo, most of us are like butter scraped over too much bread. Unfortunately, the bread is not even our own, but someone else's. Very few have taken the time to take their lives into their own hands.

It was social and cultural to live our lives on other people's terms, just one generation ago. And many millennials are perpetuating this process simply because it's the only worldview we've been taught.

However, there is a growing collective-consciousness that with a lot of work and intention, you can live every moment of your life on your own terms.

You are the designer of your destiny.

You are responsible.

You get to decide. You *must* decide—because if you don't, someone else will. Indecision is a bad decision.

With this short morning routine, your life will quickly change.

It may seem like a long list. But in short, it's really quite simple:

- Wake up
- Get in the zone
- Get moving
- Put the right food in your body
- Get ready
- Get inspired
- Get perspective

- Do something to move you forward

Let's begin:

1. Get A Healthy 7+ Hours of Sleep

Let's face it: sleep is just as important as eating and drinking water. Despite this, millions of people do not sleep enough and experience insane problems as a result.

The National Sleep Foundation (NSF) conducted surveys revealing that at least 40 million Americans suffer from more than 70 different sleep disorders; furthermore, 60 percent of adults, and 69 percent of children, experience one or more sleep problems a few nights or more during a week.

In addition, more than 40 percent of adults experience daytime sleepiness severe enough to interfere with their daily activities at least a few days each month—with 20 percent reporting problem sleepiness a few days a week or more.

On the flip side, getting a healthy amount of sleep is linked to:

- Increased memory
- Longer life
- Decreased inflammation
- Increased creativity
- Increased attention and focus
- Decreased fat and increased muscle mass with exercise
- Lower stress
- Decreased dependence on stimulants like caffeine

- Decreased risk of getting into accidents
- Decreased risk of depression

And tons more... Google it.

The rest of this article is worthless if you don't make sleep a priority. Who cares if you wake up at 5 a.m. if you went to bed three hours earlier?

You won't last long.

You may use stimulants to compensate, but that isn't sustainable. In the long run, your health will fall apart. The goal needs to be long-term sustainability.

2. Prayer and Meditation to Facilitate Clarity and Abundance

After waking from a healthy and restful sleep session, prayer and meditation are crucial for orienting yourself toward the positive. What you focus on expands.

Prayer and meditation facilitate intense gratitude for all that you have. Gratitude is having an abundance mindset. When you think abundantly, the world is your oyster. There is limitless opportunity and possibility for you.

People are magnets. When you're grateful for what you have, you will attract more of the positive and good. Gratitude is contagious.

Gratitude may be the most important key to success. It has been called the mother of all virtues.

If you start every morning putting yourself in a space of gratitude and clarity, you will attract the best the world has to offer, and not get distracted.

3. Hard Physical Activity

Despite endless evidence of the need for exercise, only one-third of American men and women between the ages of 25 to 64 years engage in regular physical activity according to the Center for Disease Control's National Health Interview Survey.

If you want to be among the healthy, happy and productive people in the world, get in the habit of regular exercise. Many people go immediately to the gym to get their body moving. I have lately found that doing yard work in the wee hours of the morning generates an intense inflow of inspiration and clarity.

Whatever your preference, get your body moving.

Exercise has been found to decrease your chance of depression, anxiety and stress. It is also related to higher success in your career.

If you don't care about your body, every other aspect of your life will suffer. Humans are holistic beings.

4. Consume 30 Grams of Protein

Donald Layman, professor emeritus of nutrition at the University of Illinois, recommends consuming at least 30 grams of protein for breakfast. Similarly, Tim Ferriss, in his book, The 4-Hour Body, also recommends 30 grams of protein 30 minutes after awaking.

According to Mr. Ferriss, his father did this and lost 19 pounds in one month.

Protein-rich foods keep you full longer than other foods because they take longer to leave the stomach. Also, protein keeps blood-sugar levels steady, which prevent spikes in hunger.

Eating protein first decreases your white carbohydrate cravings, which are the types of carbs that get you fat. Think bagels, toast and donuts.

Mr. Ferriss makes four recommendations for getting adequate protein in the morning:

- Eat at least 40% of your breakfast calories as protein
- Do it with two or three whole eggs (each egg has about six grams of protein)
- If you don't like eggs, use something like turkey bacon, organic pork bacon or sausage, or cottage cheese
- Or, you could always do a protein shake with water

5. Take a Cold Shower

Tony Robbins starts every morning by jumping into a 57-degree Fahrenheit swimming pool.

Why would he do such a thing?

Cold water immersion radically facilitates physical and mental wellness. When practiced regularly, it provides long-lasting changes to your body's immune, lymphatic, circulatory and digestive systems that improve the quality of your life. It can also increase weight loss because it boosts your metabolism.

A 2007 research study found that taking cold showers routinely can help treat symptoms of depression often more effectively than prescription medications. That's because cold water triggers a wave of mood-boosting neurochemicals, which make you feel happy.

There is, of course, an initial fear of stepping into a cold shower. Without a doubt, if you've tried this before, you have found yourself standing outside the shower dreading the thought of going in.

You may have even talked yourself out of it and said, "Maybe tomorrow." And turned the hot water handle before getting in.

Or, maybe you jumped in but quickly turned the hot water on?

What has helped me is thinking about it like a swimming pool. It's a slow painful death to get into a cold pool slowly. You just need to jump in. After 20 seconds, you're fine.

It's the same way with taking a cold shower. You get in, your heart starts beating like crazy. Then, after 20 seconds, you feel fine.

To me, it increases my willpower and boosts my creativity and inspiration. While standing with the cold water hitting my back, I practice slowing my breath and calm down. After I've chilled out, I feel super-happy and inspired. Lots of ideas start flowing and I become motived to achieve my goals.

6. Listen to/Read Uplifting Content

Ordinary people seek entertainment. Extraordinary people seek education and learning. It is common for the world's most successful people to read at least one book per week. They are constantly learning.

I can easily get through one audiobook per week by just

listening during my commute to school and while walking on campus.

Taking even 15–30 minutes every morning to read uplifting and instructive information changes you. It puts you in the zone to perform at your highest.

Over a long enough period of time, you will have read hundreds of books. You'll be knowledgeable on several topics. You'll think and see the world differently. You'll be able to make more connections between different topics.

7. Review Your Life Vision

Your goals should be written down — short term and long term. Taking just a few minutes to read your life vision puts your day into perspective.

If you read your long-term goals every day, you will think about them every day. If you think about them every day, and spend your days working toward them, they'll manifest.

Achieving goals is a science. There's no confusion or ambiguity to it. If you follow a simple pattern, you can accomplish all of your goals, no matter how big they are.

A fundamental aspect of that is writing them down and reviewing them every single day.

8. Do at Least One Thing Toward Long-Term Goals

Willpower is like a muscle that depletes when it is exercised. Similarly, our ability to make high quality decisions becomes fatigued over time. The more decisions you make, the lower quality they become — the weaker your willpower.

Consequently, you need to do the hard stuff first thing in the morning. The important stuff.

If you don't, it simply will not get done. By the end of your day, you'll be exhausted. You'll be fried. There will be a million reasons to just start tomorrow. And you will start tomorrow—which is never.

So your mantra becomes: The worst comes first. Do that thing you've been needing to do. Then do it again tomorrow.

If you take just one step toward your big goals every day, you'll realize those goals weren't really far away.

Conclusion

After you've done this, no matter what you have for the rest of your day, you'll have done the important stuff first. You'll have put yourself in a place to succeed. You'll have inched toward your dreams.

Because you'll have done all these things, you'll show up better in life. You'll be better at your job. You'll be better in your relationships. You'll be happier. You'll be more confident. You'll be more bold and daring. You'll have more clarity and vision.

Your life will shortly change.

You can't have mornings like this consistently without waking up to all that is incongruent in your life. Those things you despise will meet their demise. They'll disappear and never return.

You'll quickly find you're doing the work you're passionate about.

Your relationships will be passionate, meaningful, deep and fun!

You will have freedom and abundance.

The world, and the universe, will respond to you in beautiful ways.

3

Humans Are Holistic Systems: Your Physical Health Affects Everything

Human beings are holistic—when you change a part of any system you simultaneously change the whole. You can't change a part without fundamentally changing everything.

Every pebble of thought—no matter how inconsequential—creates endless ripples of consequence. This idea, coined the butterfly effect by Edward Lorenz came from the metaphorical example of a hurricane being influenced by minor signals—such as the flapping of the wings of a distant butterfly—several weeks earlier. Little things become big things.

When one area of your life is out of alignment, every area of your life suffers. You can't compartmentalize a working system. Although it's easy to push certain areas—like your health and relationships—to the side, you unwittingly infect your whole life. Eventually and always, the essentials you procrastinate or avoid will catch up to your detriment.

Conversely, when you improve one area of your life, all other areas are positively influenced. As James Allen wrote in *As a Man Thinketh*, "When a man makes his thoughts pure, he no longer desires impure food."

We are holistic systems.

Humanity as a whole is the same way. Everything you do effects the whole world, for better or worse. So I invite you to ask:

"Am I part of the cure? Or am I part of the disease?" — Coldplay

Stop Consuming Caffeine

Although people think they perform better on caffeine, the truth is, they really don't. Actually, we've become so dependent on caffeine that we use it to simply get back to our status-quo. When we're off it, we underperform and become incapable.

Isn't this absurd?

With healthy eating, sleeping, and exercise, your body will naturally produce far more and better energy than caffeine could ever provide. Give it up and see what happens. You will probably get withdrawal headaches. But after a few days, you'll feel amazing.

Stop Consuming Refined Sugar

If you stop consuming sugar, your brain will radically change. Actually, study after study is showing that refined sugar is worse for our brains than it is for our waistlines. According to Dr. William Coda Martin, refined sugar is nothing more than poison because it has been depleted of its life forces, vitamins and minerals.

Refined sugar has now been shown to make us cranky, make us make rash decisions, and make us stupid.

Again, like caffeine, if you stop eating refined sugar, you will experience some negative withdrawals. But, like any good habit, the effects of this will be seen in the long-run. What would your health be like a year from now (or five) if you were completely refined sugar-free?

Fast From All Food and Caloric Beverages 24 Hours Once Per Week

One-day (24-hour) food fasts are a popular way to maintain health and vigor. Fasting leverages the self-healing properties of the human body. Radical health improvements occur when the digestive system is given rest and the organs get ample time to repair and heal themselves.

A regular practice of fasting can:

- Improve digestive efficiency
- Increase mental clarity
- Increase physical and mental vigor
- Remove toxins
- Improve vision
- Give a general feeling of well being

Like all the other habits, fasting gets easier with practice. I've been fasting for years and it's one of the best things I have done for my health.

Fasting is also one of the most recognized techniques in religious and spiritual practices. I also use fasting to get spiritual clarity and refinement.

Honestly, I could go on for hours about this one. Give it a try. You'll never be the same.

Consume a Tablespoon of Coconut Oil Once Per Day

Coconut oil is one of the healthiest foods on the planet.

Here are 7 reasons you should eat coconut oil every single day:

- It boosts HDL (good) cholesterol and simultaneously blocks LDL (bad) cholesterol buildup
- It has special fats that help you burn more fat, have more energy, and maintain healthy weight
- It fights aging and keeps you looking and feeling young
- It reduces fever and acts as an anti-inflammatory
- It is antibacterial and thus wards off possible illnesses
- It improves memory and cognitive functioning (even for people with Alzheimer's)
- It can boost testosterone for men and balance healthy hormones level for both men and women

Coconut oil is a healthy alternative to caffeine. Eating a small amount will give you a shot of energy without the side-effects.

Buy a Juicer and Juice a Few Times Per Week

Juicing is an incredible way to get loads of vitamins and nutrients from fruits and vegetables. These nutrients can:

- Help protect against cardiovascular disease, cancer and various inflammatory diseases
- Guard against oxidative cellular damage from everyday cellular maintenance and exposure to chemicals and pollution.

There are several approaches you can take to juicing. You can reset your body by doing a 3-10 day juice "cleanse." Or, you could simply incorporate juice into your regular diet. I do both from time to time.

I always feel enormously better after juicing. Especially when I get lots of intense greens like kale into my system.

Drink 64-100 Ounces of Water Per Day

Human beings are mostly water. As we drink healthy amounts of water, we have smaller waistlines, healthier skin, and better functioning brains. Actually, as we drink enough water, it's safe to say we're better in every way.

It's a no-brainer. If you're not drinking the healthy amount of water each day, you should critically assess your priorities in life.

Floss Your Teeth

About 50 percent of Americans claim to floss daily. My guess is that's a large over-estimate. Either way, the benefits of flossing are incredible.

Doing so daily prevents gum disease and tooth loss. Everyone gets plaque, and it can only be removed by flossing or a deep cleaning from your dentist. Plaque buildup can lead to cavities, tooth decay, and gum disease. If left untreated, gum disease can be a risk factor for heart disease, diabetes, and a high body mass index.

Yes, not flossing can make you fat.

Not only that, but it greatly reduces bad breath.

4

Ordinary People Seek Entertainment, Extraordinary People Seek Education

Ordinary people seek entertainment. Extraordinary people seek education and learning. It is common for the world's most successful people to read at least one book per week. They are constantly learning.

I can easily get through one audiobook per week by just listening during my commute to school and while walking on campus. Taking even 15-30 minutes every morning to read uplifting and instructive information changes you. It puts you in the zone to perform at your highest.

Over a long enough period of time, you will have read hundreds of books. You'll be knowledgeable on several topics. You'll think and see the world differently. You'll be able to make more connections between different topics.

True learning is difficult, and is more than acquiring knowledge. There is a difference between knowing and understanding. You don't truly know something until you've experienced it, until you can explain it simply, and do it. I could read every book about building a computer. But until I've actually built a computer, I don't really know. Theory and lived experience are two completely different things.

So don't let your only learning be that from books. Apply what you learn from books by actually doing stuff! Make mistakes. Have experiences.

Listen to Audiobooks on 2X Speed While Taking Notes in a Journal for 30–60 Minutes Per Day

Generally, I'd recommend reading for 30–60 minutes per day. But lately, I've been listening to audiobooks or podcasts on my iPod at 2X speed while taking notes in journal. When you first try listening at 2X, it's a little weird. But you get used to it. Then, listening at normal speed feels like slow-motion.

Neurologically, when you listen to something, a different part of your brain is engaged than when you write it down. Memory recorded by listening does not discriminate important from non-important information. However, writing creates spatial regions between important and non-important pieces of information — allowing your memory to target and ingrain the important stuff you want to remember.

Furthermore, research has shown the simple act of writing something down increases brain development and memory.

It's becoming regular for me to have 15–30 pages of notes in my journal every morning during my 60 minutes of audiobook listening.

Marry Your Best Friend

"For all the productivity and success advice I've read, shaped and marketed for dozens of authors in the last decade, I've never really seen someone come out and say: Find yourself a spouse who complements and supports you and makes you better." —Ryan Holiday

Research done by economists have found—even after controlling for age, education, and other demographics—that married people make 10 to 50 percent more than single people.

Why would this be?

Being married gives you a higher purpose for being productive. You are no longer a lone ranger, but have another person who relies on you.

Marriage also smacks you in the face with what's really important in life. Sure, hanging out and partying are fun. But too many people get stuck in this phase and miss the meaning that comes from building a life with someone.

You will never find a better personal development seminar or book than marriage. It will highlight all of your flaws and weaknesses, challenging you to become a better person than you ever thought possible.

Stop Consuming the News or Reading the Newspaper

Although the amount of warfare and deaths by human hands are reducing globally, you will not get that message watching televised news or reading the newspaper.

On the contrary, these media outlets have an agenda. Their goal is to appeal to your fears by inflating extreme cases—making them seem normal and commonplace. If they didn't do so, their viewership would plummet. Which is why Peter Diamandis, one of the world's experts on entrepreneurship and the future of innovation has said, "I've stopped watching TV news. They couldn't pay me enough money."

You can get high quality news curated from Google news. When you detox from the toxic filth that is public news, you'll be startled as your worldview becomes radically more optimistic. There is no objective reality. Instead, we live in perceived realities and are thus responsible for the worldview we adopt.

5

Expanding Your Time

You Can't Have It All

Every decision has opportunity cost. When you choose one thing, you simultaneously don't choose several others. When someone says you can have it all, they are lying. They are almost certainly not practicing what they preach and are trying to sell you on something.

The truth is, you don't want it all. And even if you did, reality simply doesn't work that way. For example, I've come to terms with the fact that I want my family to be the center of my life. Spending time with my wife and three foster kids is my top priority. As a result, I can't spend 12 or 15 hours a day working like some people. And that's okay. I've made my choice.

And that's the point. We all need to choose what matters most to us, and own that. If we attempt to be everything, we'll end up being nothing. Internal conflict is hell.

Although the traditional view of creativity is that it is unstructured and doesn't follow rules, creativity usually occurs by thinking inside the proverbial box, not outside of it. People flex their creative muscles when they constrain their options rather than broaden them. Hence, the more clearly defined and constraining your life's objectives the better, because it allows you to sever everything outside those objectives.

Almost Everything In Life Is A Distraction

"You cannot overestimate the unimportance of practically everything." — Greg McKeown

Almost everything is a distraction from what really matters. You really can't put a price-tag on certain things. They are beyond a particular value to you. You'd give up everything, even your life, for those things.

Your relationships and personal values don't have a price-tag. And you should never exchange something priceless for a price.

Keeping things in proper perspective allows you to remove everything non-essential from your life. It allows you to live simply and laser focused, and to avoid dead-end roads leading nowhere.

Five Minutes Is A Lot Of Time

When you have five minutes of down-time, how do you spend that time?

Most people use it as an excuse to rest or laze.

By lazing for 5 five minute breaks each day, we waste 25 minutes daily. That's 9,125 minutes per year (25 X 365). Sadly, my guess is we're wasting far more time than that.

I was once told by my 9th grade English teacher that if I

read every time I had a break—even if the break was just for a minute or two—that I'd get a lot more reading done than expected. She was right. Every time I finished my work early, or had a spare moment, I'd pick up a book and read.

How we spend our periodic five minute breaks is a determining factor to what we achieve in our lives. Every little bit adds up.

Why can we justify wasting so much time?

Yesterday Is More Important Than Today

"The best time to plant a tree was 20 years ago. The second best time is now." —Chinese Proverb

Our present circumstances are a reflection of our past decisions. Although we have enormous power to change the trajectory of our lives here and now, we are where we are because of our past. While it's popular to say the past doesn't matter, that simply is not true.

Today is tomorrow's yesterday. What we do today will either enhance or diminish our future-present moments. But most people put things off until tomorrow. We thoughtlessly go into debt, forego exercise and education, and justify negative relationships. But at some point it all catches up. Like an airplane off-course, the longer we wait to correct the longer and harder it is to get back on-course.

Time is absolutely marvelous. We get to anticipate the experiences we want to have—which is often more enjoyable than the experiences themselves. We get to have the experiences we long for. And then we get to remember and carry those experiences with us forever. The past, present, and future are uniquely important and enjoyable.

Go to Bed Early and Rise Early

According to countless research studies, people who go to bed and rise early are better students. Harvard biologist Christoph Randler found that early sleep/risers are more proactive and are more likely to anticipate problems and minimize them efficiently, which leads to being more successful in the business.

Other benefits of going to bed and rising early—backed by research—include:

- Being a better planner
- Being holistically healthier as individuals
- Getting better sleep
- More optimistic, satisfied, and conscientious

Waking up early allows you to proactively and consciously design your day. You can start with a morning routine that sets the tone for your whole day. You show self-respect by putting yourself first. In your morning morning routine, you can pray/meditate, exercise, listen to or read inspiring content, and write in your journal. This routine will give you a much stronger buzz than a cup of coffee.

Decide Where You'll Be in Five Years and Get There in Two

"How can you achieve your 10 year plan in the next 6 months?"—Peter Thiel

There is always a faster way than you originally conceive. Actually, goal-setting can slow your progress and diminish your potential if you rely too heavily upon it.

In an interview with *Success Magazine*, Tim Ferriss said that he doesn't have five or ten year goals. Instead, he works on "experiments" or projects for a 6-12 week period of time. If they do extremely well, the possible doors that could open are endless. Tim would rather play to the best possibilities than get stuck on one track. He says this approach allows him to go drastically farther than he could ever plan for.

Have No More Than 3 Items on Your To-Do List Each Day

When you shift your life from day-to-day reactivity to one of creation and purpose, your goals become a lot bigger. Consequently, your priority list becomes smaller. Instead of doing a million things poorly, the goal becomes to do a few things incredibly—or better yet, to do one thing better than anyone else in the world.

"If you have more than three priorities, then you don't have any." —Jim Collins

So, instead of trying to do a million small things, what one or two things would make the biggest impact?

Dan Sullivan, founder of Strategic Coach, explains that there are two economies: The Economy of Hard Work and The Economy of Results.

Some people think hard work is the recipe. Others think about the most efficient way to get a desired result.

Tim Ferriss, in his book, *The 4-Hour Body*, explains what he calls Minimum Effective Dose (MED), which is simply the smallest dose that will yield a desired result and anything past the MED is wasteful. Water boils at 100°C at standard air pressure—it is not "more boiled" if you add more heat.

What is the fastest way to get your desired outcome?

Fast From the Internet 24 hours Once Per Week

Your body gets an intervention when you fast. Your mind and relationships could use one too. Unplug yourself from the matrix.

If you haven't caught on already, human beings are highly addictive creatures. We love our coffee, sugar, and internet. And these things are all great. But our lives can be far more enhanced by using these tools in wisdom.

The purpose of the internet fast is to reconnect to yourself and your loved ones. So, you probably shouldn't do it the same day you do your food fast. Because eating is one of the strongest ways to form bonds.

You'll be blown away by how much more connected you feel to your loved ones when you can give them your undivided attention. It may even feel awkward for a while having a real-life conversation without looking at your phone every three minutes.

Say "No" to People, Obligations, Requests, and Opportunities You're Not Interested in From Now On

"No more yes. It's either HELL YEAH! or no."—Derek Sivers

Your 20 seconds of daily courage will most consistently involve saying "no" to stuff that doesn't really matter. But how could you possibly say "no" to certain opportunities if you don't know what you want? You can't. Like most people, you'll be seduced by the best thing that comes around. Or, you'll crumble under other people's agendas.

But if you know what you want, you'll have the courage and foresight to pass up even brilliant opportunities—because ultimately they are distractors from your vision. As Jim Collins said in *Good to Great*, "A 'once-in-a-lifetime opportunity' is irrelevant if it is the wrong opportunity."

Give At Least One Guilt-Free Hour of Relaxation Per Day

In our quest for success, many of us have become workaholics. However, relaxation is crucial for success. It is akin to resting between sets at the gym. Without resting, your workout will be far less than it could have been.

Foolishly, people approach their lives like a workout without rest breaks. Instead, they take stimulants to keep themselves going longer and longer. But this isn't sustainable or healthy. It's also bad for productivity and creativity in the short and long run.

Check Your Email and Social Media At Least 60-90 Minutes After You Wake Up

Most people check their email and social media immediately upon waking up. This puts them in a reactive state for the remainder of the day. Instead of living life on their own terms, they'd rather respond to other people's agendas.

Hence, the importance of having a solid morning routine. When you wake up and put yourself, not other people first, you position yourself to win before you ever begin playing.

> "Private victory always precedes public victory."
> –Stephen Covey

Make the first few hours of your morning about you, so that you can be the best you can for other people. My morning routine consists of prayer, journal writing, listening to audiobooks and podcasts while I workout, and taking a cold shower.

After I've had an epic morning, and I'm clear on the

direction of my day, I can utilize email and social media for my benefit rather than detriment.

Make a Few Radical Changes to Your Life Each Year

Reinvent yourself every year. Novelty is an antidote to monotony. Jump into new pursuits and relationships.

Try things you've never done before.

Take risks.

Have more fun.

Pursue big things you've been procrastinating for years.

In the past year, my wife and I went from having no kids to having three foster kids (ages 4, 6, and 8). I've started blogging. I quit my job and started writing full-time. I completely changed my diet. I've changed my entire daily routine.

Without question, this year has been the most transformative year of my life. It's taught me that you can change your whole life in one year. I plan on changing my whole life for the better *every year*.

Spend 5 Minutes Creating Outlines In Advance (This Will Save You Hours)

In his book, *Essentialism*, Greg McKeown explains a method he uses to save time and enhance creativity. Hours, or even days, before jumping into a creative activity, he spends just

3-4 minutes creating an outline. Once the outline is built, he walks away from it. When he starts into his project, the outline triggers a flood of information getting him quickly into the zone; rather than having to mentally generate all the information he needs from scratch.

I too use this method in my writing. I design writing sessions for the sole purpose of creating outlines. With a pile of outlines already structured, I can often return and write several articles in a single session. Without the outlines, I can often lose motivation and focus after just one.

I've even used this approach in outlining the contents of entire books. I take a blank sheet of paper and write all the chapters that would be in a book. With that framework in place, I can brain dump and get a solid first draft in no time.

Focus Is Today's I.Q.

We live in the most distracted era of human history. The internet is a double-edged sword. Like money, the internet is neutral — and it can be used for good or bad based on who uses it.

Sadly, most of us are simply not responsible enough for the internet. We waste hours every day staring idly at a screen. Millennials are particularly prone to distractions on the internet, but nowadays, everyone is susceptible.

Our attention spans have shrunk to almost nothing. Our willpower has atrophied. We've developed some really bad habits that often require extreme interventions to reverse.

There is a growing body of scientific evidence suggesting

the internet—with its constant distractions and interruptions—is turning us into scattered and superficial thinkers. One of the biggest challenges to constant distraction is that it leads to "shallow" rather than "deep" thinking, and shallow thinking leads to shallow living. The Roman philosopher Seneca may have put it best 2,000 years ago: "To be everywhere is to be nowhere."

In his book, *Deep Work: Rules for Focused Success in a Distracted World*, Cal Newport differentiates "deep work," from "shallow work." Deep work is using your skills to create something of value. It takes thought, energy, time and concentration. Shallow work is all the little administrative and logistical stuff: email, meetings, calls, expense reports, etc. Most people aren't moving toward their goals because they prioritize shallow work.

> *"The ability to perform deep work is becoming increasingly rare at exactly the same time it is becoming increasingly valuable in our economy. As a consequence, the few who cultivate this skill, and then make it the core of their working life, will thrive."* — Cal Newport

6

No Other Success Can Compensate for Failed Relationships

Do Something Kind for Someone Else Daily

"Have I done any good in the world today? Have I helped anyone in need? Have I cheered up the sad and made someone feel glad? If not, I have failed indeed. Has anyone's burden been lighter today, because I was willing to share? Have the sick and the weary been helped on their way? When they needed my help was I there?"—Will L. Thompson (music and text)

If we're too busy to help other people, we've missed the mark. Taking the time to spontaneously—as well as planned—helping other people is one of the greatest joys in life. Helping others opens you up to new sides of yourself. It helps you connect deeper with those you help and humanity in general. It clarifies what really matters in life.

As Thomas Monson has said, "Never let a problem to be solved become more important than a person to be loved." That would truly be a failure.

Say "Thank you" Every Time You're Served by Someone

It's amazing when you meet someone who is expressively and genuinely grateful. It's amazing because, frankly, it's rare.

I remember one day while working as a busser of a restaurant as a teenager. Every time I went by a certain table, whether I was refilling waters, bringing food, anything… the kid at the table (no more than 20 years old) graciously said "thank you." I even heard him from close proximity saying it to all the other employees when they stopped by his table.

This experience had a dramatic impact on me. It was so simple what he was doing. Yet, so beautiful. I instantly loved this person and wanted to serve him even more.

I could tell by how he looked in my eyes when saying "thank you" that he meant it. It came from a place of gratitude and humility.

Interestingly, one study has found that saying "thank you," facilitated a 66 percent increase in help offered by those serving. Although altruism is the goal, don't be surprised as your habit of graciously saying "thank you" turns into even more to be thankful for.

Say "I Love You" 3+ Times a Day to the Most Important People in Your Life

According to neuroscience research, the more you express love (like gratitude), the more other people feel love *for you*. Sadly, people are taught absurd mindsets about being vulnerable and loving in relationships. Just this morning, my wife and I had to coax and prod our three foster kids to say one nice thing about each other, and to say they loved each other.

It took several minutes for our 8 year old foster boy to muster the strength to say he loved his sister. Yet, all of our kids constantly berate and belittle each other.

You know the feeling: when you want to say "I love you" but hold back. What a horrible feeling.

Why do we hesitate to express our love?

Why do we hesitate to connect deeply with others?

This may be strange, but if you tell your friends and family you love them, *they'll be blown away*. I once knew a Polynesian missionary who told everyone he loved them. It was clear he was sincere.

I asked him why he did it. What he told me changed my life. "When I tell people I love them, it not only changes them, but it changes me. Simply by saying the words, I feel more love for that person. I've been telling people all around me I love them. They feel treasured by me. Those who know me have come to expect it. When I forget to say it, they miss it."

"The bitterest tears shed over graves are for words left unsaid and deeds left undone." –Harriet Beecher Stowe

Genuinely Apologize to People You've Mistreated

People make mistakes several times every single day.

Sadly—and hilariously—much of the time we act like kids and blame our mistakes on external factors. Research has found that people who don't openly and often apologize experience higher levels of stress and anxiety.

You don't need that pent-up energy in your life. Make amends and let it go. It's not your choice if people choose to forgive you.

Make Friends with Five People Who Inspire You

> *"You are the average of the five people you spend the most time with."*—Jim Rohn

Who you spend time with is incredibly important. Even more fundamental is: what types of people are you *comfortable* around?

Your comfort level is one of the clearest indicators of your character. Are the people you enjoy being around inspiring or degrading, hard-working or lazy?

What kinds of beliefs do you friends have?

What kinds of goals are they pursuing?

How much money do they make?

What does their health look like?

All of these things dramatically impact you. And it is one of the most painful experiences in the world to *become uncomfortable* around people who have long been your friends. When you grow and evolve and long for more, you'll begin seeking a different crowd to surround yourself with.

Misery loves company. Don't let them hold you back. Move on but never detach from the love you have for those people.

Be Spontaneously Generous with a Stranger At Least Once Per Month

Life isn't all about what you can achieve or acquire. It's more about who you become and what you contribute.

Interestingly, research done at Yale has found that people are instinctively cooperative and generous. However, if you stall and think about being helpful or generous, you're less likely to do it. And the longer you wait, the likelihood of you being helpful diminishes.

So, be spontaneous. When you get the wild thought of buying the person's food in the car behind you, just do it. Don't think about it.

If you're driving down the road and see someone with car trouble off to the side, just do it. Don't think about it.

When you want to say "I love you," to a loved one, just do it. Don't think about it.

Paralysis by analysis is dumb. And Malcolm Gladwell explains in *Blink* that snap-decisions are often far better than well-thought out ones.

Write and Place a Short, Thoughtful Note for Someone Once Per Day

The messages of handwritten letters impact deeper and are

remembered longer than electronic messages. There is no comparison to this traditional form of conversation. Handwritten messages are so powerful that people often keep these notes for a long time. Sometimes a lifetime.

Jack Canfield has taught that writing 3-5 handwritten notes per day will change your relationships. In our email world, it can seem inefficient to hand-write and mail a letter. But relationships aren't about efficiency.

Not only will handwriting letters change your relationships, it will change you. Research has shown that writing by hand increases brain development and cognition more than typing can.

Consequently, the things you write will be seared into your own memory as well, allowing both you and the recipient to reflect back on cherished moments.

Writing handwritten notes spices up your relationships, adding an element of fun. It's exciting placing kind and loving notes in random places for your loved ones to find. Put a note under the windshield wipers of your loved one's car to find after a hard day's' work. Hidden, wait til they come out and watch them from across the street. You'll see their eyes light up and smile spread.

Other fun places include:

- In the fridge
- In the closet
- On the computer keyboard
- In their shoe
- In their wallet
- The mail box

Anywhere that makes the experience a surprise…

Become Good Friends With Your Parents

Many people have horrible relationships with their parents. I once did myself. Growing up can be tough and sometimes are parents make horrible decisions that negatively impact us.

However, my parents have become my best friends. They are my confidants. I turn to them for wisdom and advice. They understand me like no one else. Biology is a powerful thing.

Although I don't see things the same way my parents do, I love them and respect their viewpoints. I love working out with my dad and talking about big ideas with my mom.

I couldn't imagine not being close to them.

If your parents are still around, rekindle those ties or increase the flame. You'll find enormous joy in those relationships.

Eat At Least One Meal with Your Family Per Day

If possible, eat a sit-down meal with your loved ones daily. It doesn't matter if it's breakfast, lunch, or dinner.

We've become so high-paced in the world that everything we do is on the go. We've forgotten what it means to just be with our loved ones.

Eating together creates a sense of community like nothing else.

Teens who have fewer than three family dinners a week are

3.5 times more likely to have abused prescription drugs and to have used illegal drugs other than marijuana, three times more likely to have used marijuana, more than 2.5 times more likely to have smoked cigarettes, and 1.5 times more likely to have tried alcohol, according to the CASA report.

Never Forget Where You Came From

It's easy when you achieve any level of success to believe you are solely responsible for that success. It's easy to forget where you came from.

It's easy to forget all the sacrifices other people have made to get you where you are. It's easy to see yourself as superior to other people. Burn all your bridges and you'll have no human connection left. In that internal cave of isolation, you'll lose your mind and identity, becoming a person you never intended to be.

Humility, gratitude, and recognition of your blessings keeps your success in proper perspective. You couldn't do what you've without the help of countless other people. You are extremely lucky to be able to contribute in the way you have.

7

Think and Grow Rich

Define what Wealth and Happiness Mean to You

"Be everything to everybody and you'll be nothing for yourself."—John Rushton

No two human beings are the same. So why should we have one standard of success? Seeking society's standard of success is an endless rat-race. There will always be someone better than you. You'll never have the time to do *everything*.

Instead, you recognize that every decision has opportunity cost. When you choose one thing, you simultaneously don't choose several others. And that's okay. Actually, it's beautiful because we get to choose our ultimate ideal. We must define success, wealth, and happiness in our own terms because if we don't, society will for us—and we will always fall short. We'll always be left wanting. We'll always be stuck comparing ourselves and competing with other people. Our lives will be an endless race for the next best thing. We'll never experience contentment.

Change the Way You Think, Feel, and Act About Money

Most people have an unhealthy relationship with money. It's not necessarily their fault; it's what they were taught.

In order to change your financial world, you need to alter your paradigm and feelings about money.

Here are some key beliefs the most successful people in the world have:

- In a free-market economy, anyone can make as much money as they want.
- Your background, highest level of education, or IQ is irrelevant when it comes to earning money.
- The bigger the problem you solve, the more money you make.
- Expect to make lots of money. Think BIG: $100,000, $500,000, or why not $1 million?
- What you focus on expands. If you believe in scarcity, you'll have little.
- If you believe there is unlimited abundance, you'll attract abundance.
- When you create incredible value for others, you have the right to make as much money as you want.
- You're not going to be discovered, saved, or made rich by someone else. If you want to be successful, you have to build it yourself.

When you develop a healthy relationship, you will have more.

You won't spend money on the crap most people waste their money on. You'll focus more on value than price.

One Dollar Is A Lot Of Money

I was recently in Wal-Mart with my mother-in-law buying a few groceries. While we were in the check-out line, I pointed an item out to her I thought was interesting (honestly can't remember what it is anymore). What stuck out to me is that she said, "One dollar. That's a lot of money!"

Why this surprised me is that my in-laws are not short of money. Actually, this happened while we were on a family trip (30+ people) at Disney World — the whole thing being paid for by them.

Understanding the value of one dollar is the same as coming to appreciate the value of time. To thoughtlessly spend one dollar may not seem like a big deal, but it actually is. That frivolous spending compounded over a long enough time could be millions.

And the truth is, most millionaires are "self-made", 80 percent being first-generation rich, and 75 percent being self-employed. Not getting paid hourly challenges you to take more responsibility for every minute and every dollar. Consequently, a great majority of millionaires are extremely frugal — or at least highly mindful — with their money.

Retirement Should Never Be The Goal

"To retire is to die." — Pablo Casals

The most powerful way to punch someone in the face is to aim a foot behind their face. That way, you have full momentum and power when you make contact. If you aim only for the face itself, by the time you reach it you'll have already begun slowing down. Thus, your punch will not be as powerful as you intended it to be.

Retirement is the same way.

Most people planning for retirement begin slowing down in their 40's and 50's. The sad part is, as momentum-based beings, when you begin to slow down, you start a hard-to-reverse decaying process.

Research has found that retirement often:

- Increases the difficulty of mobility and daily activities
- Increases the likelihood of becoming ill
- And decreases mental health

But retirement is a 20th century phenomena. And actually, the foundations undergirding this outdated notion make little sense in modern and future society.

For instance, due to advances in health care, 65 is not considered old age anymore. When the Social Security system was designed, the planners chose age 65 because the average lifespan was age 63 at the time. Thus, the system was designed only for those who were really in need, not to create a culture of people being supported by others' labor.

Furthermore, the perception that people over 65 can't provide meaningful work no longer makes sense either. Retirement became a thing when most work was manual labor—but today's work is more knowledge-based. And if there's anything lacking in today's society, its wisdom, people in their later years have spent a lifetime refining.

Retirement should never be the goal. We are fully capable to work—in some capacity—until our final breath.

My 92 year old grandfather, Rex, was a fighter pilot in WWII. In the past five years he's written three books. He goes to bed every night at 8 P.M. and wakes up every morning at 4:30 A.M. He spends the first 2.5 hours of his day watching inspirational and instructional content on television. He then eats breakfast at 7 A.M. and spends his day reading, writing, connecting and serving people, and even doing physical labor around his son's (my dad's) house. He even walks around his neighborhood proselyting his faith and asking random strangers how he can help them.

I have no intention of stopping or slowing down. Contrary to popular belief, humans are like wine and get better with age.

You Earn As Much Money As You Want To

Most people "say" they want to be successful. But if they really wanted to, they'd be successful.

I used to tell people, "I wish I played the piano." Then someone said, "No you don't. If you did, you'd make the time to practice." I've since stopped saying that, because he was right.

Life is a matter of priority and decision. And when it comes to money—in a free-market economy—you can make as much money as you choose. The question is, how much money do you really want to make?

Instead of vegging on social media day-after-day, year-after-year, you could spend an hour or two each day building something of value—like yourself.

In the book, *Think and Grow Rich*, Napoleon Hill invites readers to write down on a piece of paper the amount of money they want to make, and to put a time-line on it. This single act will challenge you to think and act in new ways to create the future of your wanting.

For example, despite growing up so poor that for a time his family lived in their Volkswagen van on a relative's lawn, Jim Carrey believed in his future. Every night in the late 1980's, Carrey would drive atop a large hill that looked down over Los Angeles and visualize directors valuing his work. At the time, he was a broke and struggling young comic.

One night in 1990, while looking down on Los Angeles and dreaming of his future, Carrey wrote himself a check for $10 million and put in the notation line "for acting services rendered." He dated the check for Thanksgiving 1995 and stuck it in his wallet. He gave himself five years. And just before Thanksgiving of 1995, he got paid $10 million for *Dumb and Dumber*.

Earning Money Is Moral

> *"For better or worse, humans are holistic. Even the human body does best when its spiritual and physical sides are synchronized... People's bodies perform best*

when their brains are on board with the program... Helping your mind to believe what you do is good, noble, and worthwhile in itself helps to fuel your energies and propel your efforts."—Rabbi Daniel Lapin

I know so many people who genuinely believe making money is immoral, and that people with money are evil. They believe those who seek profits force those weaker than them to buy their products.

Money is not evil, but neutral. It is a symbol of perceived value.

If I'm selling a pair of shoes for $20 and someone decides to buy them, they perceive the shoes to be worth more than the $20, or they wouldn't buy them. I'm not forcing them to buy my shoes. It's their choice. Thus, value exchange is win-win and based purely on perception. Value is subjective! If you offered that same person $20 for the shoes they just bought, they probably wouldn't sell them. They see them as worth more than $20. But what if you offered $30? They still might not sell them.

There is no "correct" price for goods and services. The correct price is the perceived worth from the customer. If the price is too high, the customer won't exchange their money for it.

We are extremely lucky to live in a society with a system of money. It allows us to borrow, lend, and leverage. Our ability to scale our work would be enormously limited in a bartering and trading system.

Earning money is a completely moral pursuit when it is

uone with honesty and integrity. In fact, if you don't feel moral about the work you're doing, you should probably change your job.

When you believe in the value you provide so much that you are doing people a disservice by not offering them your services, you're on track to creating colossal value. Our work should be a reflection of us. It's always their choice whether they perceive the value in what we're offering or not.

Save 10 Percent or More of Your Income

"I would have saved 10 percent automatically from my paycheck by direct deposit into a savings account earning the best possible interest compounded daily. I would have also disciplined myself to deposit 10 percent of any additional money from gifts, refunds or other earned income. I would have bought a small house outright with the money I had saved (instead of renting an apartment for over 30 years). I would have found a job that I loved and devoted my life to it. At least you could be happy even if you were not where you wanted to be financially. Hope this helps someone out there." —D. Lorinser

Tithing yourself is a core principle of wealth creation. Most people pay *other people* first. Most people live above their means.

In total, American consumers owe:

- $11.85 trillion in debt

- An increase of 1.4% from last year
- $918.5 billion in credit card debt
- $8.09 trillion in mortgages
- $1.19 trillion in student loans
- An increase of 5.9% from last year

The U.S. Census in 2010 reported that there were 234.56 million people over the age of 18 years old, suggesting the average adult owes $3,761 in revolving credit to lenders. Across the average household, American adults also owe $11,244 in student loans, $8,163 on their autos, and $70,322 on their mortgage.

Simply switching to home-brewed coffee will save you an average of $64.48 per month (or $2 per day) or $773.80 per year. By putting the savings into a mutual fund with average earnings of 6.5% interest and reinvesting the dividends into more mutual funds over a decade, the $64.48 saved every month would grow into $10,981.93.

Tithe or Give 10 Percent of Your Income Away

> *"One gives freely, yet grows all the richer."*—Proverbs 11:24

Many of the wealthiest people in the world attribute their healthy financial life and abundance to *giving some of it away*.

Most people are trying to accumulate as much as they can. However, a natural principle of wealth creation is generosity.

As Joe Polish has said, "The world gives to the givers and takes from the takers."

From a spiritual perspective, everything we have is God's (or the Earth's). We are merely stewards over our possessions. When we die, we don't take our money with us. So why hoard it?

As you give generously and wisely, you'll be stunned by the increases in your earning potential. You'll develop traits needed for radical wealth creation.

Buy a Small Place Rather than Rent

Unless you live in a big city (which many of you do), I'm baffled how many people pay outlandish amounts on rent each month.

When my wife and I moved to Clemson to begin graduate school, we did a lot of front end work to ensure we'd be able to buy a home. What's shocking is that our mortgage payment is far less than most of our friend's rent payments. By the end of our four years here in Clemson, we'll have earned several thousand dollars in equity and even more in appreciation. Conversely, many of our friends are simply dumping hundreds of dollars into someone else's pockets every month.

Paying rent is like working hourly. You get money while you're on the clock. When you're not on the clock, you get no money. Earning equity is like having residual income. Every month you pay down your mortgage, you actually keep that money. So you're not "spending to live" like most people do.

You're living for free while saving—often earning in appreciation.

Invest Only in Industries You are Informed About

Warren Buffett doesn't invest in technology because he doesn't understand it. Instead, he invests in banking and insurance. He's not a tech guy. He invests in what he understands.

Yet, so many people invest in things they don't understand. I've made that mistake. I once invested several thousand dollars in an overseas rice distribution. Although the investment sounded incredible on paper, it's turned out to be a disaster.

I didn't have the understanding to make an informed decision. I put my trust in someone else's hands. And no one cares about your success more than you do.

From now on, I'm going to responsibly invest in things I can make informed decisions on.

Create an Automated Income Source that takes Care of the Fundamentals

We live in unprecedented times. It has never been easier to create automated income streams. No matter your skill-set and interests, you can put a business in place that runs 24/7 even while you're sleeping, sitting on the beach, or playing with your kids.

An entrepreneur is someone who works for a few years like

no one will so they can live the rest of their life like no one else can.

If you want to free up your time and energy for the things that matter most, either invest in stuff you're informed on (e.g., real estate, businesses, mutual funds), or, create a business that doesn't require you (e.g., create an online educational course about something you're passionate about).

Have Multiple Income Streams (The More the Better)

Most people's income comes from the same source. However, most wealthy people's income comes from multiple sources. I know people with hundreds of income streams coming in each month.

What would happen if you set things up so you were getting income from 5 or 10 different places each month?

What if several of those were automated?

Again, with a few short years of intentional and focused work, you can have several income streams.

Part 2

Developing the Ability to Consciously Design Your Ideal Future

8

This Is How You Train Your Brain To Get What You Really Want

Approximately six months ago, I got serious about my goal to become a professional writer. I had written an eBook and was anxious to know how to traditionally publish it.

I decided literary agents would be my best source of advice. After all, they know the publishing industry back-and-forth—or so I thought. After talking to 5-10 different agents about their coaching programs, it became apparent my questions would need to be answered elsewhere.

One particular conversation sticks out.

In order to even be considered by agents and publishers, writers need to already have a substantial readership (i.e., a platform). I told one of the agents my goal was to have 5,000 blog subscribers by the end of 2015. She responded, "That would not be possible from where you currently are. These things take time. You will not be able to get a publisher for 3-5 years. That's just the reality."

"Reality to who?" I thought as I hung up the phone.

Never Ask Advice From...

In his book, *The Compound Effect*, Darren Hardy said, "Never ask advice of someone with whom you wouldn't want to trade places."

As I pondered this quote, I realized I was asking the wrong types of people for advice. I needed to turn to people who had actually walked where I wanted to walk. Anyone can provide nebulous theory. We spend our entire public education learning theory from people who have rarely "walked the walk." As Jack Black said in *School of Rock*, "Those who can't do, teach." Similarly, there is an endless supply of content being published everyday by people who rarely practice the virtues they preach.

Contrary to theory, which cannot get you very far in the end, people who have actually been "there" provide practical steps on what you need to do (e.g., here are the five things you should focus on and forget everything else).

Why You Need To Know What You Want

> *"This is a fundamental irony of most people's lives. They don't quite know what they want to do with their lives. Yet they are very active."* —Ryan Holiday

Most kids go to college without a clue why they are there. They are floating along waiting to be told what to do next. They haven't seen or thought enough to know what their ideal life would look like. So how could they possibly know how to distinguish good advice from bad?

Conversely, people who know what they want in life see the world differently. All people selectively attend to things that interest or excite them. For example, when you buy a new car, you start to notice the same car everywhere. How does this happen? You didn't seem to notice that everyone drove Malibus before.

Our brains are constantly filtering an unfathomable amount of sensory inputs: sounds, smells, visuals, and more. Most of this information goes consciously unrecognized. Our focused attention is on what we care about. Thus, some people only notice the bad while others see the good in everything. Some notice people wearing band shirts, while others notice anything fitness related.

So, when you decide what you want, it's like buying a new car. You start seeing it everywhere—especially your newsfeeds!

What are you seeing everywhere? This is perhaps the clearest reflection of your conscious identity.

The Magical Things That Happen When You Begin Paying Attention

"How can you achieve your 10 year plan in the next 6 months?" –Peter Thiel

Wherever it is you want to go, there is a long and conventional path; and there are shorter, less conventional approaches. The conventional path is the outcome of not paying attention. It's what happens when you let other people dictate your direction and speed in life.

However, once you know what you want—and it intensely arouses your attention—you will notice simpler and easier solutions to your questions. What might have taken 10 years in a traditional manner takes only a few months with the right information and relationship.

> *"When the student is ready the teacher will appear."*
> —Mabel Collins

When I decided I was serious about becoming a writer, the advice from the literary agents couldn't work for me. I was ready for the wisdom of people who were where I wanted to be. My vision was bigger than the advice I was getting.

Around this same time and out of nowhere, I came across an online course about guest blogging. It must have popped in my newsfeeds because of my previous searching. I paid the $197, went through the course, and within two weeks was getting articles featured on multiple self-help blogs.

Within two months of taking the course, I wrote a blog post that blew up. Tim Ferriss has said, "One blog post can change your entire life." This principle holds true of anything you do. One performance, one audition, one interview, one music video, one conversation… Thus, the focus should be on quality rather than quantity.

Two months after being told it would take 3-5 years to have a substantial following, I was there. When you know what you want, you notice opportunities most people aren't aware of.

You also have the rare courage to seize those opportunities without procrastination.

Courage doesn't just involve saying "Yes"—it also involves saying, "No." But how could you possibly say "No" to certain opportunities if you don't know what you want? You can't. Like most people, you'll be seduced by the best thing that comes around.

But if you know what you want, you'll be willing to pass up even brilliant opportunities because ultimately they are distractors from your vision. As Jim Collins said in Good to Great, "A 'once-in-a-lifetime opportunity' is irrelevant if it is the wrong opportunity."

"Once-in-a-lifetime" opportunities (i.e., distractors) pop up everyday. But the right opportunities will only start popping up when you decide what you want and thus, start selectively attending to them. Before you know it, you'll be surrounded by a network you love and by mentors showing you the fastest path.

Conclusion

Ralph Waldo Emerson once said, "Once you make a decision, the universe conspires to make it happen." This quote is completely true. Once you know what you want, you can stop taking advice from just anyone. You can filter out the endless noise and hone in on your truth.

Eventually, you can train your conscious mind to only focus on what you really want in life. Everything else gets outsourced and forgotten by your subconscious.

Decide what you want or someone else will.
You are the designer of your destiny. What will it be?

9

Mental Creation Always Precedes Physical Creation

Your Vision Of Who You Want To Be Is Your Greatest Asset

> "Create the highest, grandest vision possible for your life, because you become what you believe." — Oprah Winfrey

No matter where you are right now, you can have any future you want. But one thing is for certain, what you plant you must harvest. So, please plant with intention. Mental creation always precedes physical creation. The blueprint you design in your head becomes the life you build.

Don't let society tell you how your house should look. You are an artist and a creator. Your life can be exactly how you want it, whether or not it's considered a "mansion" by others. Home is where your heart is.

Who You Are Determines What You Can Have

There's a parable of a wealthy parent who hesitated giving their unwise child an inheritance, knowing it would undoubtedly be squandered. The parent said to the child:

"All that I have I desire to give you—not only my wealth, but also my position and standing among men. That which I have I can easily give you, but that which I am you must obtain for yourself. You will qualify for your inheritance by learning what I have learned and by living as I have lived. I will give you the laws and principles by which I have acquired my wisdom and stature. Follow my example, mastering as I have mastered, and you will become as I am, and all that I have will be yours."

Going through the motions is not enough. There isn't a check-list of things you must do to be successful. You have to fundamentally change who you are to live at a higher level. You must go from doing to being—so that what you do is a reflection of who you are, and who you're becoming. Once you've experienced this change, success will be natural.

> *"After you become a millionaire, you can give all of your money away because what's important is not the million dollars; what's important is the person you have become in the process of becoming a millionaire."* —Jim Rohn

"I fully realize that my future is bright and powerful."

Free-will is a tricky subject. Both spiritually and psychologically, the whole notion is complex and conflicting.

Do we really have free-will?

To what extent do we determine the outcomes of our lives?

The majority of psychological theories would suggest that human beings do *not* have free-will; but rather, that we are nothing more than the clashing of genes and environment—no room for consciously deciding either of those things.

In similar fashion, many religious philosophies promote a God hardly worthy of worship, who despite having the power to save all predetermines a select few—leaving the rest to spend eternity tortured without explanation or reason why.

Clearly, internal wisdom discerns both of these ideas as *wrong,* if not radically incomplete.

But is our ability to act absolutely independent? Surely not. If I were to jump off my back porch in attempts of flying, I would most certainly be acted on by gravitational forces. Indeed, there are constraints on our *freedom* to act.

However, the flexibility of those constraints is proving to be quite malleable. We can consciously change our environments. And science is even coming to grips with the fact that we can manipulate our genetic expression. Our free-will is contextual, yet we have the power to manipulate the context (including our beliefs about that context); and thus, we have limitless options regarding the course our lives take.

In the movie, *The Adjustment Bureau,* the main character

David Norris (played by Matt Damon) learns about a hidden society of "angels" (known as "the Adjustment Bureau") who ensure every person's life goes according to "the plan."

According to David's plan, he isn't supposed to be with Elise, a woman he feels an innate and deep connection toward. The members of the Adjustment Bureau do all they can to ensure David and Elise's paths don't cross. But with a touch of luck, and dogged determination, David decides he's going to have Elise regardless of what "the plan" dictates.

After risking everything to have the person he loves, David inspires a member of the Adjustment Bureau, who then takes David's case to the Chairman—the creator of each person's plan. David's determination and love inspire even the Chairman, who then makes David and Elise's "plan" blank.

The film closes with the following narration by one of the members of the Adjustment Bureau:

> "Most people live life on the path we set for them, too afraid to explore any other. But once in a while, people like you come along who knock down all the obstacles we put in your way. People who realize free-will is a gift you'll never know how to use until you fight for it. I think that's the Chairman's real plan: that one day, we won't write the plan, you will."

Brilliant things begin to happen when you take extreme ownership over your life. When you're in complete alignment with yourself, you find that God has given you the power to *choose for yourself.* And if you so choose, that God will help you along your way.

Matured at this stage, you don't need to wonder or worry about how your future will turn out. Instead, you are completely confident about certain realizations. These realizations which you decide, although not yet manifested, have *already happened*. Thus, they are as real as anything else. Your life then becomes the natural unfolding of something you've consciously created in your mind.

Choose to Have Faith in Something Bigger than Yourself, Skepticism is Easy

In the timeless book, *Think and Grow Rich*, Napoleon Hill explains that a fundamental principle of wealth creation is having faith—which he defines as visualization and belief in the attainment of desire.

> As he famously said, *"Whatever the mind can conceive and believe, the mind can achieve."*

If you don't believe in your dreams, the chances of them happening are slim to none. But if you can come to fully know the things you seek will occur, the universe will conspire to make it happen.

According to Hill (see page 49 of *Think and Grow Rich*), here's how that works:

- "Faith is the starting point of all accumulation of riches!"
- "Faith is the basis of all 'miracles' and mysteries that cannot be analyzed by the rules of science!"

- "Faith is the element that transforms the ordinary vibration of thought, created by the finite mind of man, into the spiritual equivalent."
- "Faith is the only agency through which the cosmic force of Infinite Intelligence can be harnessed and used."
- "Faith is the element, the 'chemical' which, when mixed with prayer, gives one direct communication with Infinite Intelligence."

Like expressing love, in our culture, many have become uncomfortable with ideas like faith. Yet, to all of the best business minds in recent history, faith was fundamental to their success.

Make a Bucket List and Actively Knock Items Off

Most people have it backwards—they design their ambitions around their life, rather than designing their life around their ambitions.

What are the things you absolutely must do before you die? Start there.

Then design your life around those things. Or as Stephen Covey explained in *The 7 Habits of Highly Effective People*, "Begin with the end clearly in mind."

10

Prayer, Meditation, and Visualization

"I have so much to do today that I'm going to need to spend three hours in prayer in order to be able to get it all done." — Martin Luther

Spending a good chunk of time at the beginning of your day in prayer and meditation brings clarity and perspective.

These activities help you distinguish the subtle signal from the pervasive noise all around you. Almost everything in life is a distraction. If you don't put yourself in a place of clarity and perspective at the beginning of each day, you may spend your entire day on activities taking you in the wrong direction. Prayer and meditation also facilitate radical insights and inspiration. During my morning prayer and meditation, I've gotten ideas about articles to write, and people to reach out to.

Not only that, but during my prayer and meditation, I visualize and decide the best approach to achieve my objectives (often involving reaching out to people I don't know). As a result, I have intense levels of confidence and momentum when I attack my day.

Spend Your First 10 Minutes of the Day in Prayer, Gratitude, Laughter & This Question

The first 10 minutes of your day are, without question, the most important. They set the tone for how the rest of your day will be. They reflect how you will *show up* to the world.

Will you be proactive or reactive this day?

Will you be in a hurry or purposeful?

Will you be guided and inspired, or tossed to and fro with every email, phone call, interruption, and distraction that comes your way?

Will you be in control of your time or will time be in control of you?

Will you be a leader or a victim?

Will you take risks or play safe?

Will you attract abundance or scarcity?

Will you be the recipient of luck and miracles or disappointment and disaster?

Will you move toward or away from your hopes and dreams?

Robin Sharma, author of *The Leader without a Title,* spends the first 10 minutes of his day praying, laughing, and asking himself the question: *"If this was the last day of my life, how would I spend it?"*

This question helps Sharma ensure his day is spent precisely how he feels it should be.

My first 10 minutes are spent in prayer — deeply expressing gratitude for everything in my present and future life. Additionally, I visualize myself achieving my day's top priorities, and asking God to elevate my performance in everything I do.

When I walk away from these 10 minutes, I *know* I'm in a position of abundance and power. I know I've become a magnet for incredible possibilities, and that the work I'll do this day will exceed my natural abilities.

Pray and Meditate Morning, Mid-Day, and Night

In a recent interview at the Genius Network mastermind event, Joe Polish asked Tony Robbins what he does to get focused. "Do you meditate? What do you do?" Joe asked.

"I don't know that I meditate. I don't know that I want to meditate and think about nothing," Tony responded, "My goal is clarity."

Instead of full-on meditation, Tony has a morning routine that includes several breathing exercises and visualization techniques that get him to a state of clarity and focus. For me, I use prayer and pondering (my version of meditation) as the same vehicle.

Whatever your approach, the goal should be clarity and focus. What do you want to be about today?

What few things matter most during the next 24 hours?

I've gotten the best results as my morning prayer and meditation are motivational; my afternoon prayer and meditation are strategic; and my evening prayer and meditation are evaluative and educational.

Spend 5–10 Minutes Each Day Visualizing Where You Want to Be

Michael Phelps visualized himself winning races every night before going to bed. Jim Carrey visualized himself becoming a successful actor. Amazingly, research has found that visualization is nearly as effective as actually practicing the behaviors we seek to perform.

My wife and I recently started visualizing what our lives will be like two years from now when we're done with graduate school. After we put the kids to bed, we read an uplifting book for 10 minutes, then we spend two minutes visualizing our future. After we spend two minutes visualizing our futures, we discuss what we saw. It's actually a lot of fun and has brought us closer together.

If you're going to be partners, why not co-create your future together? To me, it's the best way to remain aligned and not move in opposite directions. Mental creation *always* precedes physical creation.

When visualizing your future, don't visualizing what you *think* may happen. Rather, visualize what you *want* to happen. As Abraham Lincoln masterfully stated, "The best way to predict your future is to create it."

11

Your Daily Journal—the Gateway to Your Future

> *"The life of every man is a diary in which he means to write one story, and writes another; and his humblest hour is when he compares the volume as it is with what he vowed to make it."* —J.M. Barrie, author of *Peter Pan*

You know exactly what you want in life. But you can't seem to get there. You have all these resolves.

- You're going to get healthy.
- You're going to write that book.
- You're going to be more present with your loved ones.
- You're going to start that home-based business.
- You're going to learn another language.
- You're going to be more patient and happy.
- You're going to get out of debt.
- You're going to be more organized.
- You're going to be a better friend.
- You're going to overcome bad habits.

But the problem is: Doing these is really hard. And it gets

harder every day. Some days, it seems more realistic to just give up entirely. The whole taking one step forward and one or two steps backward pattern is getting old.

You've been telling yourself for a long time *"Today is the day!"* only to fall into old ways before the day, or if you're lucky, the week, is spent.

When there's a gap between who you are and who you intend to be, you are incongruent and unhappy. You're torn, mentally exhausted, and regretful. You always slightly feel like a fraud to yourself, and probably to the people around you.

Conversely, Gandhi has said, *"Happiness is when what you think, what you say, and what you do are in harmony."*

The Need For A Powerfully Transformative Keystone Habit

If you try to tackle everything wrong in your life, you'll quickly burn-out and quit. It's happened many times before.

Life is super busy. You don't have time to focus on a thousand different areas of your life to change. That's exhausting, and frankly, not helpful.

More effective than microscopically analyzing your sabotaging behaviors, is nailing down a "keystone" habit—which tightly locks all of your other habits in place. Without the keystone, everything falls apart.

In his book, *The Power of Habit*, Charles Duhigg describes keystone habits as, *"small changes or habits that people introduce into their routines that unintentionally carry over into other aspects of their lives."*

A person might start exercising once per week, and unknowing begins eating better and being more productive at work. She begins smoking less and showing more patience with her colleagues and loved ones. She uses her credit card less, feels less stressed, and has increased motivation toward her goals. The ingrained patterns in her brain reform and she becomes an entirely different person. *All because she started exercising once per week.*

You acquire one of these habits and *everything* in your life can change. Keystone habits spark a chain reaction of other good habits and can rapidly alter every aspect of your life.

Journal Every Day

Journaling daily is the most potent and powerful keystone habit you can acquire. If done correctly, you will show up better in every area of your life—*every* area! Without question, journaling has by far been the number one factor to everything I've done well in my life.

The problem is, most people have tried and failed at journaling several times. It's something you know you *should* do, but can never seem to pin down.

After you read this post, you'll never want to miss another day of journaling again.

Here's why:

Journaling Optimizes Your Creative Potential

Most people live their lives on other people's terms. Their days are spent achieving other people's goals and submitting to other people's agendas.

Their lives have not been consciously organized in such a way that they command every waking, and sleeping, moment of their life. Instead, they relentlessly react at every chance they get.

For example, most people wake up and immediately check their phone or email. In spare seconds, we hop on Facebook and check the newsfeed. We've become addicted to input. Or in other words, we've become addicted to reactively being guided by other people's agendas.

On the other hand, Josh Waitzkin, author of *The Art of Learning,* wakes up and immediately writes in his journal for 30 minutes.

He does this because while he's been sleeping, his subconscious mind has been brewing, scheming, problem-solving, and *learning*. So when Josh wakes up, he rushes to a quiet place and engages in a bust of intellectual and creative flow.

I recently wrote about the importance of morning routines. If I were to re-write that post now, I'd include my journal. I've been doing this the past few weeks and its re-framed my entire approach to life. Additionally, I've never before had so many creative ideas crystallize.

Creators focus on outputs rather than the general populace who focus on inputs. In their free moments, creators utilize their subconscious breakthroughs. Their days are filled with creative bursts, making them incredible at their craft.

If you want to have more creative flow in your life, stop

checking your social media and email so much. Check them once or twice per day. Detach from the addiction to numb your mind and escape reality. Instead, get lost in the creative projects you've always wanted to do.

Journaling Accelerates Your Ability To Manifest Your Goals

As part of your morning creative burst, use your journal to review and hone your daily to-do list. Review and hone your life vision and big picture goals.

As you read and re-write your goals daily, they'll become forged into your subconscious mind. Eventually, your dreams and vision will consume your inner world and quickly become your physical reality.

Journaling Creates A Springboard For Daily Recovery

People struggle drastically to detach from work. More now than ever, we fail to live presently. Our loved ones are lucky to experience a small percentage of our attention while they're with us.

However, utilizing your journal can curb this mismanagement. At the end of your work day, re-open your journal and review your to-do list from that day. If your morning journal session was excellent, you'll have likely gotten everything done you intended to do. Private victories always precede public victories.

Journal sessions are your post-work reflection time. Account to yourself what you got done that day and what needs to be moved to tomorrow. Write the things you learned and experienced.

Lastly, direct your subconscious by writing about things you want to focus on tomorrow. As you put work behind you for the evening, your subconscious will be preparing a feast for you to consume during your next morning's creative and planning session.

This end of the workday journal session need not be as long as the morning session. Greg McKeown, author of *Essentialism*, recommends writing far less than you want to — only a few sentences or paragraphs at most. This will help you avoid burnout.

A primary objective of this session is to mentally turn-off work-mode. Just as in physical training, you need to rest and recover between work days in order to get stronger.

Use this session to completely unplug and detach from work. This is your time to recover and be present with your loved ones — there is more to life than work. The higher quality your recovery, the more potent and powerful your creative sessions will be.

Journaling Generates Clarity And Congruence

This keystone habit has so much power! By journaling in the

morning and evening, you'll quickly see the incongruencies in your life.

You'll see crystal-clearly what needs to be removed and what should be included in your life. Journaling is a beautiful and powerful facilitator of self-discovery. My own journaling is how I've come to form my sense of identity and path in life.

Not only will you have more clarity about your path in life, but journaling improves your ability to make small and large decisions along the way.

On the pages of your journal will be the future world you are creating for yourself. You are the author of your life's story. You deserve to be happy. You have the power to create whatever life you want. As the designer of your world, get as detailed as you desire.

Journaling Clears Your Emotions

Several research studies have found that writing in your journal reduces stress. These benefits include:

- Reducing scatter in your life
- Increased focus
- Greater stability
- Deeper level of learning, order, action, and release
- Holding thoughts still so they can be changed and integrated
- Releasing pent-up thoughts and emotions
- Empowerment
- Bridging inner thinking with outer events
- Detaching and letting go of the past

- Allowing you to re-experience the past with today's adult mind

When you are in an intensely emotional mood, journaling can help you more fully experience and understand those emotions.

After you've vented on the pages of your journal, you'll quickly find a release. Objectivity will return and you'll be able to move forward.

Without a journal, intense emotional experiences can be crippling for hours, days, and even years. However, an honest and inspired journal session can be the best form of therapy — quickly returning you better and smarter than you were before.

Journaling Ingrains Your Learning

Humans are bad at retaining information. We forget most of what we read and hear. However, when you write down the things you've learned, you retain them far better. Even if you never re-read what you've written, the simple act of writing something down increases brain development and memory.

Neurologically, when you listen to something, a different part of your brain is engaged than when you write it down. Memory recorded by listening does not discriminate important from non-important information. However, writing creates spatial regions between important and non-important pieces of information—allowing your memory to target and engrain the important stuff you want to remember.

Furthermore, the act of writing allows your subconscious mind to work out problems in unique ways, intensifying the learning process. You'll be able to work out problems and get insights while you ponder and write about the things you're learning.

Journaling Increases Your Gratitude

Even if you start a journal session in a bad mood, the insight writing brings has a subtle way of shifting your mind towards gratitude.

When you start writing what you're grateful for, new chambers of thought open in the palace of your mind. You'll often need to put your pen down and take a few overwhelming breathes. You'll be captivated not only by the amazing things in your life, but by the awe and brilliance of life in general.

As part of your morning and post-work journaling sessions, be sure to include some gratitude in your writing. It will change your entire life orientation from scarcity to abundance. The world will increasingly become your oyster.

Gratitude journaling is a scientifically proven way to overcome several psychological challenges. The benefits are seemingly endless. Here are just a few:

- Gratitude makes you happier
- Gratitude makes other people like you
- Gratitude makes you healthier

- Gratitude boosts your career
- Gratitude strengthens your emotions
- Gratitude develops your personality
- Gratitude makes you more optimistic
- Gratitude reduces materialism
- Gratitude increases spirituality
- Gratitude makes you less self-centered
- Gratitude increases your self-esteem
- Gratitude improves your sleep
- Gratitude keeps you away from the doctor by strengthening physiological functioning
- Gratitude lets you live longer
- Gratitude increases your energy levels
- Gratitude makes you more likely to exercise
- Gratitude helps you bounce back from challenges
- Gratitude makes you feel good
- Gratitude makes your memories happier (think of Pixar's *Inside Out*)
- Gratitude reduces feelings of envy
- Gratitude helps you relax
- Gratitude makes you friendlier
- Gratitude helps your marriage
- Gratitude makes you look good
- Gratitude deepens your friendships
- Gratitude makes you a more effective manager
- Gratitude helps you network
- Gratitude increases your goal achievement
- Gratitude improves your decision making
- Gratitude increases your productivity

Journaling Unfolds The Writer In You

I became a writer through journaling. While I was on a mission-trip, I wrote in my journal for one to two hours per day. I got lost in flow and fell in love with the writing process.

If you want to become a writer one day, start by journaling. Journaling can help you:

- Develop strong writing habits
- Help you discover your voice!
- Clear your mind and crystalizes your ideas
- Get closer to the 10,000 hours Malcom Gladwell says are required to become world-class at what you do
- Produce gems you could use in your other writing

Journaling Records Your Life History

I started journaling in 2008 after reading an article about the importance of journal writing. In the article, the author described how much journaling had changed her life. She said that after all these years, she now has 38 recorded volumes of personal and family history.

After finishing that article, I have never stopped writing in my journal. In my family room on a book shelf are 20-plus journals filled with my thoughts and experiences. I'm certain they will be cherished by my ancestors as I've cherished the writing of my loved ones who have passed on.

19 Other Benefits Of Journaling

Some other benefits of journaling include:

- Heals relationships
- Heals the past
- Dignifies all events
- Is honest, trusting, non-judgmental
- Strengthens your sense of yourself
- Balances and harmonizes
- Recalls and reconstructs past events
- Acts as your own counselor
- Integrates peaks and valleys in life
- Soothes troubled memories
- Sees yourself as a larger, important, whole and connected being
- Reveals and tracks patterns and cycles
- Improves self-trust
- Directs intention and discernment
- Improves sensitivity
- Interprets your symbols and dreams
- Offers new perspectives
- Brings things together
- Shows relationships and wholeness instead of separation

Strategies To Enhance The Experience

- Pray for inspiration before you begin

- If prayer is not your thing, meditate for 5–10 minutes to heighten your mental state
- Listen to music (I listen to either classical or dubstep depending on the output I'm trying to get)
- Write about the people in your life — you'll get breakthroughs about how to improve those relationships
- Write with confidence and power — use this to strengthen your resolves
- Write *"Today is going to be the best day of my life."* — read that over and over until you begin to believe it
- If you can't think of what to write, try writing about minute details of your day or recent history
- Or start with gratitude
- There are no rules
- Figure out the system that works for you — it takes time

Conclusion

I dare say that journaling is one of the most important things to do in your life. If done effectively, it will change *everything* in your life for the better.

You'll become the person you want to be.

You'll design the life you want to live.

Your relationships will be healthier and happier.

You'll be more productive and powerful.

Enjoy.

Part 3

Reframing Your Perceptual Reality

12

Gratitude—The Mother of All Virtues

Gratitude is the cure-all for all the world's problems. It has been called, "the mother of all virtues," by the Roman philosopher Cicero.

When you practice gratitude, your world changes. There is no objective reality. All people perceive reality as they selectively attend to things that are meaningful to them. Hence, some people notice the good while others notice the bad.

Gratitude is having an abundance mindset. When you think abundantly, the world is your oyster. There is limitless opportunity and possibility for you.

People are magnets. When you're grateful for what you have, you will attract more of the positive and good. Gratitude is contagious.

Psychological research has found that people who practice gratitude consistently report a host of benefits:

Physical

- Stronger immune systems
- Less bothered by aches and pains

- Lower blood pressure
- Exercise more and take better care of their health
- Sleep longer and feel more refreshed upon waking

Psychological

- Higher levels of positive emotions
- More alert, alive, and awake
- More joy and pleasure
- More optimism and happiness

Social

- More helpful, generous, and compassionate
- More forgiving
- More outgoing
- Feel less lonely and isolate

Gratitude may be the most important key to success. It has been called the mother of all virtues.

Gratitude During Difficult Times

Psychological research has found time and again that gratitude can help you during challenging and difficult times. In fact, Dr. Robert Emmons, one of the world's leading authorities on gratitude, argues that gratitude is not only helpful in getting through difficult times—it is *essential*.

It's important to realize that you can *be* grateful without actually *feeling* grateful. Sometimes life just sucks. And it doesn't feel good. But you can still focus on the good and eventually your feelings will follow. What you focus on expands.

Also, the goal of gratitude is not to ignore or deny the pain or difficulty you are experiencing. Rather, the goal is to acknowledge it and reframe your story about your pain and difficulty. As my wife always says, *"Crisis + times = humor…and the sooner you can laugh the less serious the crisis."* It can take a few days to reframe our story or experience. The sooner the better.

13

There is No Way to Happiness

Most people are *chasing* happiness. They believe it's on the other side of success. That you must first do or have something before you can be happy.

Shawn Achor, a prominent scholar on the science of happiness, explains that most parents, teachers, leaders, and people in general believe the following about happiness:

"If I work harder, I'll be more successful. If I'm more successful, then I'll be happy."

The problem with this approach, Achor says, is that it's "scientifically broken and backwards."

Every time your brain has a success, you change the goalpost of success. For example, you get good grades, now you need better grades—you made a good income, now you need a bigger income. Every time you hit a target, the target moves. Thus, "if happiness is on the opposite side of success, your brain never gets there. We've pushed happiness over the cognitive horizon as a society," says Achor.

But our brain works in the opposite order. If you can be positive and happy in the present, you'll actually show up better in life. Thus, happiness is what actually leads to success. No the other way around.

Stop trying to pursue happiness. You'll never get there.

Instead, deploy strategies that will increase your brain positivity *now*. When your brain is positively positioned, you have an increased flow of dopamine which makes you happier and increases all the learning centers of your brain (e.g., creativity, problem solving, etc.).

Scientifically, the following behaviors have been found to create lasting positive change to your brain functioning:

- Write down three *new* things you're grateful for each day. This will change your selective attention toward the positive in the world rather than the negative.
- Journaling about one positive experience you've had that day allows you to relive it.
- Exercising everyday teaches you that your behaviors matter — and that they dramatically impact you and those around you.
- Meditating each day helps you overcome the cultural ADHD of constant distraction. It helps you focus on what's really important.
- Random or conscious acts of kindness every single day. This could be as simple as sending a kind email to someone, smiling, or giving a compliment.

By spending just two minutes per day on each these activities for 21 days, you can rewire your brain toward the positive. As a result, you will live from a more optimistic and creative approach.

There Is No Way To Happiness

"There is no way to happiness—happiness is the way."—Thich Nhat Hanh

Most people believe they must:

- First have something (e.g., money, time, or love)
- Before they can do what they want to do (e.g., travel the world, write a book, start a business, or have a romantic relationship)
- Which will ultimately allow them to be something (e.g., happy, peaceful, content, motivated, or in love).

Paradoxically, this *have*—*do*—*be* paradigm must actually be reversed to experience happiness, success, or anything else you desire.

- First you be whatever it is you want to be (e.g., happy, compassionate, peaceful, wise, or loving)
- Then you start doing things from this space of being.
- Almost immediately, what you are doing will bring about the things you want to have.

We attract into our lives what we are.

For example, Scott Adams, the creator of the famous comic series Dilbert, attributes his success to the use of positive affirmations. 15 times each day, he wrote the sentence on a piece of paper, "I Scott Adams, will become a syndicated cartoonist."

The process of writing this 15 times a day buried this idea

deep into his subconscious—putting Adams' conscious mind on a treasure hunt for what he sought. The more he wrote, the more he could see opportunities before invisible to him. And shortly thereafter, he was a highly famous syndicated cartoonist. It couldn't not happen.

I personally apply a similar principle but write my goal in present tense. For example, rather than saying, "I will become a syndicated cartoonist," I write, "I am a syndicated cartoonist." Writing it in the present tense highlights the fact that you are being who you want to be, which will then inform what you do and ultimately who you become.

It's Never As Good As You Think It Will Be

"One of the enemies of happiness is adaptation," says Dr. Thomas Gilovich, a psychology professor at Cornell University who has studied the relationship between money and happiness for over two decades.

"We buy things to make us happy, and we succeed. But only for a while. New things are exciting to us at first, but then we adapt to them," Gilovich further states.

Actually, savoring the anticipation or idea of a desired outcome is generally more satisfying than the outcome itself. Once we get what we want—whether that's wealth, health, or excellent relationships—we adapt and the excitement fades. Often, the experiences we're seeking end up being underwhelming and even disappointing.

I love watching this phenomena in our foster kids. They feel like they need a certain toy or the universe will explode. Their whole world revolves around getting this one thing. Yet, once we buy the toy for them, it's not long before the joy fades and they want something else.

Until you appreciate what you currently have, more won't make your life better.

It's Never As Bad As You Think It Will Be

Just as we deceive ourselves into believing something will make us happier than it will, we also deceive ourselves into believing something will be harder than it will.

The longer you procrastinate or avoid doing something, the more painful (in your head) it becomes. However, once you take action, the discomfort is far less severe than you imagined. Even to extremely difficult things, humans adapt.

I recently sat on a plane with a lady who has 17 kids. Yes, you read that correctly. After having eight of her own, her and her husband felt inspired to foster four siblings whom they later adopted. A few years later, they took on another five foster siblings whom they also adopted.

Of course, the initial shock to the system impacted her entire family. But they're handling it. And believe it or not, you could handle it too… if you had to.

The problem with dread and fear is that it holds people back from taking on big challenges. What you will find — no matter how big or small the challenge — is that you will adapt to it.

When you consciously adapt to enormous stress, you evolve.

You Have Enough Already

In an interview at the annual Genius Network Event in 2013, Tim Ferriss was asked, "With all of your various roles, do you ever get stressed out? Do you ever feel like you've taken on too much?"

Ferriss responded, "Of course I get stressed out. If anyone says they don't get stressed out they're lying. But one thing that mitigates that is taking time each morning to declare and focus on the fact that 'I have enough.' I have enough. I don't need to worry about responding to every email each day. If they get mad that's their problem."

Ferriss was later asked during the same interview, "After having read The 4-Hour Workweek, I got the impression that Tim Ferriss doesn't care about money. You talked about how you travel the world without spending any money. Talk about the balance and ability to let go of caring about making money."

Ferriss responded, "It's totally okay to have lots of nice things. If it is addiction to wealth, like in Fight Club, 'The things you own end up owning you,' and it becomes a surrogate for things like long-term health and happiness — connection — then it becomes a disease state. But if you can have nice things, and not fear having them taken away, then it's a good thing. Because money is a really valuable tool."

If you appreciate what you already have, than more will be a good thing in your life. If you feel the need to have more to compensate for something missing in your life, you'll always be left wanting — no matter how much you acquire or achieve.

14

Rapid Goal Achievement

How You Set Up The Game Is More Important Than The Game Itself

"People may spend their whole lives climbing the ladder of success only to find, once they reach the top, that the ladder is leaning against the wrong wall." — Thomas Merton

Too many people are playing the wrong game — a losing game from the onset — and it hurts like hell. It's how you ruin your life without even knowing it.

More important than playing "the game" is how the game is set up. How you set up the game determines how you play. And it's better to win first, then play.

How does this work?

Start from the end and work backwards. Rather than thinking about what's plausible, or what's expected, or what makes sense — start with what you want. Or as Covey put it in 7 Habits, "Begin with the end clearly in mind." Once that's nailed down, then dictate the daily, weekly, monthly, and yearly behaviors that will facilitate that.

Jim Carrey wrote himself a $10 million check. Then he set out to earn it. He won the game first, then played. So can you.

Become Unstoppable at Setting & Achieving Your Goals (and "Experiments")

You can achieve any goals you want, no matter how big. *Seriously.*

There is no right or wrong way to approach goal-setting, but science confirms that certain approaches are better than others.

Here's what you need to know:

- The more clearly defined your goal, the more likely you will achieve it
- Write it down in detail
- Write it again
- Write it 15 times every day and in present tense (e.g., I *am* the President of the United States)
- Make your goal public to add some "positive pressure"
- Give your goal a time-line. According to Parkinson's Law, people fill the time allotted to them. So if you have a lot of time, you'll waste it. If you have a short amount of time, you'll get to it.
- According to psychological research, it takes 66 days to form a habit. So, do your goal every day for two months, then it will take care of itself and stop requiring so much willpower.

Although common wisdom would suggest having long-term goals, projecting your future more than a few years is little more than guesswork. Actually, to live at the razor's edge of his potential, Tim Ferriss doesn't have long-term goals. Instead, he does 3-6 month "experiments," which he puts all of his energy into. He has no clue what doors may open as a result of these experiments, so why make long-term plans? He'd rather respond to the brilliant and best opportunities that arise, taking him in now unforeseen directions.

I've recently adopted Ferriss' concept of doing short-term experiments. This has changed my approach to my work. For example, a few months ago I stumbled upon a personal development article that had been shared over 1,000,000 times on social media. I decided to perform an experiment to attempt creating an article that would also get 1,000,000 shares. The result was a nearly 8,000 word article called, "50 Ways Happier, Healthier, And More Successful People Live On Their Own Terms."

Although the article wasn't shared a million times, the results were profound and unexpected. An editor at *TIME* asked if they could syndicate the article. Additionally, the article brought several thousand new readers (including some of my heroes) and subscribers to my blog. Lastly, it brought on several new coaching clients.

That was just one short experiment that took a week to perform. Experiments are a fun way to pursue goals because they allow you to get innovative and bold. Because experiments are short-term — and thus relatively low risk — they should be "moon shots."

Why play small?

So take your goal and 10X it. Make it audacious and even absurd. If it doesn't excite and even scare you, you're playing too small. If you 10X your vision, don't neglect 10X'ing your effort — which means *over*estimating what would be required to achieve your goal.

What's the worst that could happen? You waste a few months and learn a lot while doing it?

Do Something Every Day that Terrifies You

"A person's success in life can usually be measured by the number of uncomfortable conversations he or she is willing to have."—Tim Ferriss

But you don't have to constantly be battling your fears. Actually, Darren Hardy has said that you can be a coward 99.9305556% of the time (to be exact). You only need to be courageous for 20 seconds at a time.

Twenty seconds of fear is all you need. If you courageously confront fear for 20 seconds every single day, before you know it, you'll be in a different socio-economic and social situation.

Make that call.

Ask that question.

Pitch that idea.

Post that video.

Whatever it is you feel you want to do–do it. The anticipation of the event is far more painful than the event itself. So just do it and end the inner-conflict.

In most cases, your fears are unfounded. As Seth Godin has explained, our comfort zone and our safety zone are not the same thing. It is completely safe to make an uncomfortable phone call. You are not going to die. Don't equate the two.

Recognize that most things outside your comfort zone are completely safe.

Start Before You're Ready

In a recent interview with *Success Magazine,* Marie Forleo told Darren Hardy that one of the keys to becoming successful is starting before you feel ready. Get experience. Make mistakes. Stop thinking about it.

Throwing yourself into the fire is the fastest way to learn and adapt to something. You're immediately exposed and naked. You're forced to quickly learn on your feet.

But most people hide until they *feel* ready—which is far after they should've started. "Perfectionism" leads to procrastination and often never *doing* or trying. Paralysis by analysis.

No more analyzing. Learn as you go. Then you're learning will have concrete context rather than abstract guessing. You'll never *feel* ready. You get ready through engaging in an activity—by getting your hands dirty—not by *thinking* about it.

"*Every day you say 'No' to your dreams, you might be pushing back your dreams a whole 6 months; a whole year. That one single day. That one day you didn't get up could have pushed your stuff back, I don't know how long.*"—Eric Thomas in Unbroken

Make Your Bed First Thing in the Morning

According to psychological research, people who make their bed in the morning are happier and more successful than those who don't. If that's not enough, here's more:

- 71 percent of bed makers consider themselves happy
- While 62 percent of non-bed-makers are unhappy
- Bed makers are also more likely to like their jobs, own a home, exercise regularly, and feel well rested
- Whereas non-bed-makers hate their jobs, rent apartments, avoid the gym, and wake up tired.

Crazy, right?

Something so simple. Yet, when you make your bed first thing in the morning, you knock-off your first accomplishment of the day. This puts you in a mindset of "winning."

Do it! It only takes 30 seconds.

Make One Audacious Request Per Week (What Do You Have to Lose?)

"Rainmakers generate revenue by making asks. They ask for donations. They ask for contracts. They ask for deals. They ask for opportunities. They ask to meet with leaders or speak to them over the phone. They ask for publicity. They come up with ideas and ask for a few minutes of your time to pitch it. They ask for help. Don't let rainmaking deter you from your dream. It's one of the barriers to entry, and you can overcome it. Once you taste the sweet victory of a positive response, you'll not only become comfortable with it, you might even enjoy it. But making asks is the only way to bring your dream to life."—Ben Arment

I got into graduate school way after applications were due because I asked.

I've gotten free NBA tickets by asking a few players I saw at a hotel.

I've gotten my work published on high tier outlets because I ask.

Very few things in life are just randomly given to you as an adult. In most cases, you need to earn it and/or ask for it.

Yet, there are many opportunities currently available to everyone if they would muster the courage and humility to ask.

The entire crowdfunding industry is based on making asks.

Start making bold and audacious asks. What's the worst that could happen? They say "No"?

What's the best that could happen?

When you don't ask, you lose by default. And you'll never know the opportunities you missed out on.

Don't sell yourself short. Ask that beautiful girl on a date. Ask for that raise or big opportunity at work. Ask people to invest in your idea.

Put yourself out there. You'll be blown away by what happens.

If Your Goals Are Logical, Don't Expect Luck (or the like)

"You need to aim beyond what you are capable of. You need to develop a complete disregard for where your abilities end. If you think you're unable to work for the best company in its sphere, make that your aim. If you think you're unable to be on the cover of Time magazine, make it your business to be there. Make your vision of where you want to be a reality. Nothing is impossible." — Paul Arden

Most people's goals are completely logical. They don't require much imagination. They certainly don't require faith, luck, magic, or miracles.

Personally, I believe it's sad how skeptical and secular many people are becoming. I find great pleasure in having faith in the spiritual. It provides context for life and meaning for personal growth. Having faith allows me to pursue that which others would call absurd, like walking on water and transcending death. Truly, with God all things are possible. There is absolutely nothing to fear.

Leverage Your Position

No matter how small your wins along the way are, leverage your position!

You have a high school diploma? Leverage your position!

You know a guy who knows a guy who knows a guy? Leverage your position!

You get an article featured on some unknown blog? Leverage your position!

You have $100? Leverage your position!

Sadly, most people can't stop looking at the other side of the fence. They fail to realize the brilliant possibilities currently available to them. This is bad stewardship.

There are people you already know who have information you need.

There are people you already know who have capital you can use.

There are people you already know who can connect you with people you should know.

Instead of wanting more, how about you utilize what you already have?

Until you do, more won't help you. Actually, it will only continue hurting you until you learn to earn something for yourself. It's easy to want other people to do it for you. But real success comes when you take ownership of your life. No one else cares more about your success than you do.

Your current position is ripe with abundant opportunity. Leverage it. Once you gain another inch of position, leverage it for all it's worth. Don't wish for more. Wish you were better. And soon enough, you'll find yourself in incredible positions and collaborating with your heroes.

Success is based on choice.

Success is based on having and maintaining a motivation worth fighting for.

It's based on believing what others might call a fantasy. It's based on leveraging your position and maintaining the momentum of every step you take.

15

How to Create Enormous Value in the Work You Do

You Have Every Advantage To Succeed

It's easy to talk about how hard our lives are. It's easy to talk about how unfair life is. And that we got the short-end of the stick. But does this kind of talking really help anyone?

When we judge our situation as worse than someone else's, we are ignorantly and incorrectly saying, "You've got it easy. You're not like me. Success should come easy to you because you haven't had to deal with what I've gone through."

This paradigm has formally become known as the victim mentality, and it generally leads to feelings of entitlement.

The world owes you nothing. Life isn't meant to be fair. However, the world has also given you everything you need. The truth is, you have every advantage in the world to succeed. And by believing this in your bones, you'll feel an enormous weight of responsibility to yourself and the world.

You've been put in a perfect position to succeed. Everything in the universe has brought you to this point so you can now shine and change the world. The world is your oyster. Your natural state is to thrive. All you have to do is show up.

Competition Is The Enemy

"All failed companies are the same: they failed to escape competition." — Peter Thiel

Competition is extremely costly to maximum product reach and wealth creation. It becomes a battle of who can slightly out-do the other for cheaper and cheaper. It's a race to the bottom for all parties involved.

Instead of trying to compete with other people or businesses, it's better to do something completely novel or to focus on a tightly defined niche. Once you've established yourself as an authority over something, you can set your own terms — rather than reactively responding to the competition. Thus, you want to monopolize the space in which you create value.

Competing with others leads people to spend every day of their lives pursuing goals that aren't really their own — but what society has deemed important. You could spend your whole life trying to keep up, but will probably have a shallow life. Or, you can define success for yourself based on your own values and detach yourself from the noise.

If You Need Permission To Do Something, You Probably Shouldn't Do It

My father-in-law is a highly successful real-estate investor. Throughout his career, he's had hundreds of people ask him if they should "go into real-estate." He tells every one of them the same thing: that they shouldn't do it. In fact, he actually tries talking most of them out of it. And in most cases he succeeds.

Why would he do that?

"Those who are going to succeed will do so regardless of what I say," my father-in-law told me.

I know so many people who chase whatever worked for other people. They never truly decide what they want to do, and end up jumping from one thing to the next — trying to strike quick gold. And repetitively, they stop digging just a few feet from the gold after resigning the spot is barren.

No one will ever give you permission to live your dreams. As Ryan Holiday has said in *The Obstacle is the Way*, "Stop looking for angels, and start looking for angles." Rather than hoping for something external to change your circumstances, mentally reframe yourself and your circumstances.

> *"When you change the way you see things, the things you see change."* — Wayne Dyer

You are enough.

You can do whatever you decide to do.

Make the decision and forget what everyone else says or thinks about it.

Don't Seek Praise. Seek Criticism.

As a culture, we've become so fragile that we must combine honest feedback with 20 compliments. And when we get feedback, we do our best to disprove it. Psychologists call this confirmation bias — the tendency to search for, interpret, favor, and recall information that confirms our own beliefs, while giving excessively less consideration to alternative possibilities.

It's easy to get praise when you ask family and friends who will tell you exactly what you want to hear. Instead of seeking praise, your work will improve if you seek criticism.

How could this be better?

You will know your work has merit when someone cares enough to give unsolicited critique. If something is noteworthy, there will be haters. As Robin Sharma, author of *The Monk Who Sold His Ferrari*, has said, "haters confirm greatness." When you really start showing up, the haters will be intimidated by you. Rather than being a reflection of what they could do, you become a reflection of what they are not doing.

The World Gives To The Givers And Takes From The Takers

From a scarcity perspective, helping other people hurts you because you no longer have the advantage. This perspective sees the world as a giant pie. Every piece of the pie you have is pie I don't have. So in order for you to win, I must lose.

From an abundance perspective, there is not only one pie, but an infinite number of pies. If you want more, you make more. Thus, helping others actually helps you because it makes the system as a whole better. It also builds relationships and trust and confidence.

I have a friend, Nate, who is doing some really innovative stuff at the real estate investing company he works for. He's using strategies that no one else is using. And he's killing it. He told me he considered keeping his strategies a secret. Because if other people knew about them, they'd use them and that'd mean less leads for him.

But then he did the opposite. He told everyone in his company about what he was doing. He has even been giving tons of his leads away! This has never been seen before in his company.

But Nate knows that once this strategy no longer works, he can come up with another one. And that's what leadership and innovation is all about. And people have come to trust him. Actually, they've come to rely on him for developing the best strategies.

Nate makes pies — for himself and several other people. And yes, he is also the top-selling and highest-earning in his company. It's because he gives the most and doesn't horde his ideas, resources, or information.

Create Something You Wish Already Existed

Many entrepreneurs design products to "scratch their own itch." Actually, that's how loads of problems are solved. You experience a difficulty and create a solution.

Musicians and artists approach their work the same way. They create music they'd want to listen to, draw painting they'd want to see, and write books they wish were written.

That's how I personally approach my work. I write articles I myself would want to read.

Your work should first and foremost resonate with yourself. If you don't enjoy the product of your work, how can you expect other people to?

Don't Look For The Next Opportunity

The perfect client, perfect opportunity, and perfect circumstances will almost never happen. Instead of wishing things were different, why not cultivate what's right in front of you?

Rather than waiting for the next opportunity, the one in your hands is the opportunity. Said another way, the grass is greener where you water it.

I see so many people leave marriages because they believe better relationships are "out" there. In most cases, these people start new relationships and end them the same way the previous relationship ended. The problem isn't your circumstances. The problem is you. You don't find your soul-mate, you create your soul-mate through hard work.

> *"Don't wish it was easier wish you were better. Don't wish for less problems wish for more skills. Don't wish for less challenge wish for more wisdom."*–Jim Rohn

Don't Wait To Start

If you don't purposefully carve time out every day to progress and improve — without question, your time will get lost in the vacuum of our increasingly crowded lives. Before you know it, you'll be old and withered — wondering where all that time went.

As Harold Hill has said — "You pile up enough tomorrows, and you'll find you are left with nothing but a lot of empty yesterdays."

I waited a few years too long to actively start writing. I was waiting for the right moment when I'd have enough time, money, and whatever else I thought I needed. I was waiting until I was somehow qualified or had permission to do what I wanted to do.

But you are never pre-qualified. There is no degree for "Live your dreams."

You qualify yourself by showing up and working. You get permission by deciding.

Life is short.

Don't wait for tomorrow for something you could do today. Your future self will either thank you or shamefully defend you.

Don't Publish Too Early

At age 22, Tony Hsieh (now CEO of Zappos.com), graduated from Harvard. When Tony was 23 years old, six months after starting Linkexchange, he was offered one million dollars for the company. This was amazing to Tony because less than a year before, he was stoked to get a job at Oracle making 40K per year.

After much thought and discussion with his partner, he rejected the offer believing he could continue to build Linkexchange into something bigger.

His true love is in building and creating. A true pro gets paid, but doesn't work for money. A true pro works for love.

Five months later, Hsieh was offered 20 million dollars from Jerry Yang, cofounder of Yahoo!. This blew Tony away. His first thought was, "I'm glad I didn't sell five months ago!" However, he held his cool and asked for a few days to consider the proposal. He would make this decisions on his terms.

He thought about all the things he would do if he had all that money, knowing he would never have to work another day in his life. After reflecting, he could only devise a small list of things he wanted:

- A condo
- A TV and built-in home theatre
- The ability to go on weekend mini-vacations whenever he wanted
- A new computer
- To start another company because he loves the idea of building and growing something.

That was it.

His passion and motivation wasn't in having stuff. He concluded that he could already afford a TV, a new computer, and could already go on weekend mini-vacations whenever he wanted. He was only 23 years old, so he determined a condo could wait. Why would he sell Linkexchange just to build and grow another company?

A year after Tony rejected the 20 million dollar offer,

Linkexchange exploded. There were over 100 employees. Business was booming. Yet, Hsieh no longer enjoyed being there. The culture and politics had subtly changed in the process of rapid growth. Linkexchange was no longer Hsieh and a group of close friends building something they loved. They had hired a bunch of people in a hurry who didn't have the same vision and motivations they had. Many of the new employees didn't care about Linkexchange, or about building something they loved. Rather, they just wanted to get rich quick—purely self-interested.

So he decided to sell the company on his terms. Microsoft purchased Linkexchange in 1998 for 265 million dollars when Hsieh was 25 years old.

A similar concept emerged in a conversation I recently had with Jeff Goins, best-selling author of *The Art of Work*. I asked his advice about publishing a book I want to write and he said, "Wait. Don't jump the gun on this. I made that mistake myself. If you wait a year or two, you'll get a 10x bigger advance, which will change the trajectory of your whole career."

Here's how it works. With 20K email subscribers, a writer can get around a $20–40K book advance. But with 100–200K email subscribers, a writer can get around a $150–500K book advance. Wait a year or two and change the trajectory of your career (and life).

This isn't about procrastination. It's about strategy. Timing—even a few seconds—could change your whole life.

If You Can't Solve A Problem, It's Because You're Playing By The Rules

"There is nothing that is a more certain sign of insanity than to do the same thing over and over and expect the results to be different." — Albert Einstein

Convention is where we're at. Breaking convention is how we'll evolve, which requires a gargantuan quantity of failure.

If you don't have the grit to fail 10,000 times, you'll never invent your lightbulb. As Seth Godin has said, "If I fail more than you do, I win."

Failure is something to be prized and praised. Failure is feedback. Failure is moving forward. It's conscious and exerted effort toward something you've never done before. It's incredible.

> "The person who doesn't make mistakes is unlikely to make anything."–Paul Arden

Your Work Should Be A Performance

The cool part about poetry is that to most poets, how their poems are performed is just as important — if not more important — than what is actually said.

In a similar way, when you go to an event or to hear a speech, you're usually going to see the speaker, not hear what they have to say. You already know what they have to say.

No matter what type of work you are in, it will be better received if you see it as an art-form. You are performing for an audience. They want you just as much as they want your work — often more.

You Get To Decide How It Works

Ryan Holiday, author of *The Obstacle is the Way*, explains what he calls "the moment," which every skilled creative has experienced. "The moment," is when your eyes are opened to the mechanics and behind-the-scenes of your craft.

Until you have this moment, it all seems like magic to you. You have no idea how people create what they create. After you have this moment, you realize that everything is done by a person intentionally creating a particular experience.

I was recently watching *Lord of the Rings* and it dawned on me that those movies would be completely different if they weren't directed by Peter Jackson. Completely different!

Every shot, every set, the lighting, the costumes, how the characters and landscapes look, and how the whole film feels and is portrayed. It all would have looked and felt completely different based on the experience a different director was trying to create.

Thus, there is no right or wrong way. Rather, it's about doing things your way. Until you experience this "moment," you'll continue attempting the correct or best way to do things. You'll continue copying other people's work.

But if you persist, you'll become disillusioned to those who were once your idols. They are people just like you and me. They've just made a decision to create in their own way.

The idea of imitation will become abhorrent, freeing you to

create as you see fit. You'll emerge with your own voice and original work. You'll be less troubled about how your work is received and more focused on creating something you believe in.

The Music You Listen To Determines Your Success In Life

"Without music, life would be a mistake" — Friedrich Nietzsche

One study found that the type of music you listen to affects how you perceive neutral faces. If you listen to sad music, you're more likely to interpret people being sad. By listening to positive music, you're more likely to see happy faces which will influence how you interact with people.

Listening to moderate noise level makes our mental processing slightly more difficult, which leads us to utilize more creative methods of problem solving. When that music is ambient, we can delve deeper into the wellsprings of neural creativity.

Other research found that your music preference reflects your personality type. For example, they found that classical music fans tend to have high self-esteem, are creative, introvert and at ease; and that chart pop fans tend to have high self-esteem, are hardworking, outgoing and gentle, but are not creative and not at ease.

Science highlights the fact that in some cases, silence is not golden. For instance, listening to classical music enhanced the visual attention of stroke patients while listening to nothing at all worsened attention. Other research found that cyclists who listened to music required seven percent less oxygen than those listening to nothing. Indeed, music can literally change our entire energy, emotion, and motivation in an instant. It's a powerful and beautiful tool.

You can also use music as a trigger for optimal performance. For example, Michael Phelps had a routine he did religiously before each swimming event involving music. He's not alone. Many athletes use music before events to trigger relaxation from the pressure and even to psych themselves up.

When asked by *Time Magazine* about his use of music prior to races, Phelps said it kept him focused and helped him "tune everything out, and take one step at a time." When asked about the kind of music he listens to, he answered, "I listen to hip hop and rap." Interestingly, research has found that high tempo music like hip hop can create strong arousal and performance readiness. Other evidence finds the intensity of the emotional response can linger long after the music has stopped. So, while Phelps is in the water swimming, he's still hyped from his hip hop.

Lastly, research has found that the types of music we listen to impact our level of spirituality. This last point is particularly important to me.

Spirituality heavily influences everything I do, from how I interact with my family, to what and how I write, to how I develop and pursue my goals. In order to being spiritually aware, I've stopped listening to music with negative tones and lyrics. I usually listen to classical, new wave stuff like

Enya, and ambient/electrical stuff like Ryan Farish. I also have some electro/dub step stuff that gets my creativity flowing. The following songs are ones I've listened to on repeat while writing.

- Club Soda by Ghostland Observatory
- Echoes by Digitalism
- Da hype by Junior Jack
- This cover of Ellie Goulding is also highly repeatable
- Fragile by Daft Punk
- Rain by Blackmill
- The Morning Room by Helios
- Dive by Tycho (whole album) — more on the ambient/electro side (anything Tycho is good)
- Lick It by Kaskade & Skrillex (ICE Mix) — ambient/electro
- Discipleship by Teen Daze (most of Teen Daze is good) — Also really love Morning House
- Modern Driveway by Luke Abbott
- Zoinks by Session Victim

Hopefully something in there is enjoyable and just distracting enough to blow up your creativity bubbles.

16

Self-Acceptance Is The Counterintuitive Way To Become The Best Version Of Your Self

Jeremy Piven, the actor famous for his roles in Entourage and Mr. Selfridge, was recently interviewed by Success Magazine. In the interview, he mentioned that, as an actor, the only way to get work is to audition for specific roles. There's just no way around that tried and true ritual.

The challenge for most actors and actresses? They get in their own way. It doesn't matter how much homework they've done for the audition. It doesn't matter how talented they are. If they are so set on getting a part, they fail at one of the key aspects of auditioning: being present, which is the essence of flow. Thus, they come across as desperate and scattered; and it manifests in lackluster performances before an auditioning committee.

It was only when Piven quit worrying about the outcome that he was able to audition successfully. He came across more natural and spontaneous. He quit trying to be what he thought others wanted him to be; and instead allowed his art to be a gift without attached contingencies. If he didn't get the gig, either they didn't "get it," or it just wasn't the right fit. He could then move on to the next audition without over-analyzing his performance. This shift in approach and motivation allowed him to get the jobs he always wanted.

Piven is not alone. For the first six seasons of American Ninja Warrior, not a single person completed all of the stages. However, Isaac Caldiero recently became the first American Ninja Warrior. In previous years, Caldiero said he put too much pressure on himself to succeed. However, this year, he just wanted to have fun and see what happened.

In a similar vein, trying to create a particular outcome while showing affection to loved ones can pull you from the now and comes off as inauthentic. People can sense phoniness, especially when it comes to love.

As Leo Buscaglia, world renowned researcher and speaker on love, has said, "Love is always bestowed as a gift—freely, willingly and without expectation. We don't love to be loved; we love to love."

It's so easy to forget that the work we do—although enjoyable to us—isn't completely about us. Our work is for and about the people we are providing it for. As Seth Godin has said, "A generous gift comes with no transaction foreseen or anticipated." Yet, Godin continues, "In most families, even the holidays are more about present exchange than the selfless act of actually giving a gift."

So, how do we live our lives without obsessing over a specific outcome? How do we live authentically and allow life to unfold organically? And how do we let love, rather than reward, be our primary motivation for everything we do?

Focus On Your Behavior And Not The Outcome

People often say, "If you want to be happier, lower your expectations." Recent research supports this notion. I've always had trouble with this idea; it always seemed to me to justify permanent mediocrity. I don't think Jeremy Piven has low expectations for his acting. Nor do I believe Isaac Caldiero expects to fail. Although low expectations may be related to happiness, they are also related to low performance. Conversely, high expectations increase performance. Both of these expectations form what appears to be a self-fulfilling prophecy.

So how do we wrap our brain around these contradictory suggestions? Do we forget the outcome, or do we set high goals for ourselves? Research has found that expectations in one's own ability serves as a better predictor of high performance than expectations about a specific outcome. In his book, "The Personal MBA," Josh Kaufman explains that when setting goals, your locus of control should target what you can control (i.e., your efforts) instead of results you can't control (e.g., whether you get the part).

Expect optimal performance from yourself and let the chips fall where they may. The organic output will be your highest quality work—which is the true reward. Put most simply: Do what is right, let the consequence follow.

Move Beyond Self-Esteem

"Care about what other people think and you will always be their prisoner."—Lao Tzu

When people try expressing their creativity, their self-esteem is often a reflection of the outcome of their work. Was it good? we ask ourselves. If it's not, we get down on ourselves. This is the essence of self-esteem—our subjective evaluation of our own worth. It is highly ego-focused and an unhealthy roller coaster experience. Thus, when we experience difficulty or failure, our self-esteem plummets. When we succeed, it skyrockets. In this way, our emphasis on our self-esteem radically hinders our ability to achieve flow.

The idea that self esteem is important has become a dogmatic assumption by people in western and highly individualized cultures. But Roy Baumeister, one of the world's most prominent psychologists, argues self-esteem causes more problems than it solves, and a waste of time in the pursuit of health and well-being, Baumeister argues.

Rather than obsessing about how you feel about yourself, you can move beyond self-esteem into a state of self-acceptance. To accept yourself unconditionally means to accept yourself even if no achievements or approvals are met. There is no rating of the self. According to psychological research, not accepting yourself can result in embarrassment, feelings of inadequacy, anxiety, and depression. None of these feelings are helpful to achieving flow.

Some may argue that self-acceptance means you're okay with mediocrity. On the contrary, you can accept who you are while still striving for more. And that's the entire point: self-acceptance allows you to actually embrace where you are on the path. You live in the moment because, come what may, you are enough and you have enough. You are blessed beyond measure.

Be Grateful For What Is

Self-acceptance and gratitude are similar concepts. Gratitude is the appreciation and acceptance of what is, whereas ingratitude is an under-appreciation of what is and a longing for what's perceived to be missing.

Having a deep sense of gratitude not only allows you to live in the moment, but can actually intensify and enhance the moment. For example, Dr. Robert Emmons explains that connecting more deeply with your body by seeing it as a brilliant gift can help you be more present as you touch, see, smell, taste, and hear—evoking enhanced consciousness and sensation.

For me, I use prayer, meditation, and journal writing to deepen my gratitude and live more presently. Having done this consistently for several years now, I've learned to see everything in my life as a gift. Every moment is gold. From this space, I can enjoy the moment for what it is without respect for what it might become. Thus, flow becomes natural and easy.

Conclusion

Flow is an optimal conscious state where you feel and perform at your highest level. You become completely absorbed in what you're doing—pure presence. Everything else in the world falls away into utter insignificance as your sense of self dissolves into a higher realm of connection. Every action you perform flows seamlessly into the next. You live 100 percent unscripted, and in the moment.

To make flow a regular and fluid experience in your life, let go of your attachments to specific outcomes. This does not mean you don't have goals or ambitions. Rather, these ambitions don't define you. And more importantly, they don't consume your mind while you perform.

Flow is also facilitated by accepting fully who you are, and the work you feel inspired to do. Hold nothing back. Be bold and vulnerable. Take risks. Trust in your higher power with whom you are fully connected.

Lastly, embrace gratitude by living fully. Feel and connect to the moment. This moment is priceless. Don't waste it by wishing it was something else. It is a gift. It is your moment.

About the Author

Benjamin and his wife, Lauren, are the foster parents of 3 epic kids. He is pursuing his PhD in Industrial and Organizational Psychology at Clemson University. His work has been featured at TIME, Psychology Today, Huffington Post, Business Insider, New York Observer, Thought Catalog, and others.

Printed in Great Britain
by Amazon